True Stories from
Mr. Nova Scotia Know-It-All
Bruce Nunn

MORE
History
with a Twist

NIMBUS
PUBLISHING

Nimbus Publishing Limited
PO Box 9166
Halifax, NS   B3K 5M8
(902) 455-4286

Printed and bound in Canada

Designer: Margaret Issenman, MGDC

FRONT COVER:
        The wrecked Patricia in front of the Brunswick Street fire station
        (Wells family photo).
        Photo of Author: Ully P. Bleil.

Canadian Cataloguing in Publication Data
        Nunn, Bruce, 1962–
        More history with a twist: true stories from Mr. Nova Scotia Know-It-All
        ISBN 1-55109-378-2
1. Nova Scotia—History. 2. Tales—Nova Scotia. I. Title.
FC2311.8.N85 2001   971.6   C2001-902177-1
F1037.6.N85 2001

The Canada Council | Le Conseil des Arts
for the Arts | du Canada

We acknowledge the financial support of the Government of Canada through the Book Publishing Industry Development Program (BPIDP) and the Canada Council for our publishing activities.

For Thomas and Adam Nunn
The two best parts
of my own story.

Photo/Illustration Credits:

Contents

Foreword

Dear Bruce,

Just after your kind invitation to scribble down a few words for this volume of "Twisted History," I was engrossed in the words of one of my favorite "Deep Thinkers," the dashing and talented Joseph Alois Schumpeter (1883-1950).

He observed in *Capitalism, Socialism and Democracy* that "... history sometimes indulges in jokes of questionable taste." Reading that phrase I was reminded of you and of your wonderful work on "Information Morning" as Mr. Nova Scotia Know-It-All. I'm not at all sure whether it has been history which has played jokes on us as we scanned the province's "back pages" or whether you have played jokes on the history of this storied province.

I do know that like many people in Nova Scotia I have looked forward to your weekly visits. They not only teach me things I didn't know about this place, but the stories usually contain some fine nugget which makes the morning's "lesson" as palatable as bacon and eggs.

In the introduction to the first volume of your stories, I mentioned how heartening it was to have a permanent record of your histories which, in radio, end up in the "ether" nano-seconds after we finish.

Let me repeat that sentiment and remark how much more attractive the permanent record is after you have polished our miscues from the final draft.

Stay Twisted.

Don Connolly

Don Connolly
Information Morning
CBC Radio One
Halifax, Nova Scotia

Introduction and Acknowledgements

(Or, "What is this and who's responsible for it?")

You know, if you had told a younger me that, at this pivotal point in my adult life, I'd be on the public airwaves every week, using a ridiculous pseudonym, telling twisted stories of people's lives, I would have said...

...Well, actually I wouldn't have had a comeback for that one. Who'd have guessed? Mr.Nova Scotia Know-It-All? How absurd. No one in their right mind would go public wearing a moniker like that. But then, about that "right mind" thing—I've never quite had one of those. Though I am grateful for my slightly slanted perspective. Somehow this twisted storyteller's stance I've taken seems to be working. Still! You are holding further proof of the wonderfully varied samples to be had from the rich story strata of Nova Scotian culture. It's just a matter of digging in the right spots, I guess. So far, so good. Behold, the sequel to History with a Twist ... More History with a Twist! (Well, what would YOU call it?)

Now, when digging, most excavators hate hitting a root. In my line of digging, I like that surprise. I follow the roots to see where they lead. Forget the vertical hole into history. Getting at the origin, the cause, the nub of the beginning of a place or a life or an event is what I enjoy. Finding, amid that dig into our past, the odd slants, the twisted connections deep down that seem somehow mysteriously more abundant in this special place than in others has been a personal joy, a rewarding journalistic challenge, and a plain fun time. Fun is important in this pursuit. Humour and history! Here, on this seabound coast, we have plenty of both, and sometimes they are all we have to get us by.

So, it's my hope that this all-new collection of Nova Scotia Know-It-All stories—originally told on CBC Radio One's Information Morning—reflects our unique storied past in all its wild splendor: dramatic, tragic, comedic, nostalgic, heroic, touching, and sometimes unexpectedly bizarre. Welcome to Nova Scotia in "Know-It-All" style.

These stories of the Bluenose province are from my ever-growing collection, originally researched from the tips and questions contributed by loyal listeners of CBC Radio in Nova Scotia, and around the world via the internet. A big thanks to all listeners and contributors.

This ain't folklore or tall tales we're talking about here. These are real stories of Nova Scotian's lives, from them and about them. Painstaking, investigative, fact-finding tactics are employed in nailing down the details. As accurate as is possible, these stories may be old but contemporary reporter-type investigations and confirmations are required. Call it historical journalism. The very latest news stories. (Sometimes a hundred years late!)

The truth is also in the telling. To that end, a hearty tip of the microphone to the skipper of the good ship Information Morning, Don Connolly, who capably guides our weekly radio chat into the channel waters so charted. Sure, sometimes we tack in unexpected directions but we eventually reach the right harbours. It's all part of the entertaining twists and turns of sailing on the (air)waves in a province where the storytelling tides are characteristically chaotic. Or maybe it's me, the unconventional sailor. Anyway, this skipper always willingly goes with the flow. Thanks Don. I raise a flag of thanks also to Elizabeth Logan, Margot Brunelle, and the rest of the Information Morning crew. From this program the Nova Scotia Know-It-All stories were first launched, some years ago. No one predicted they'd still be afloat and on such varied seas. Must be something in the water. Many of these original stories have also surfaced in *The Daily News*.

The greatest encouragement of my storytelling has come from my best audience, my two young sons. When they were little, they begged me at bedtime to drop the storybook and give them an original, pleading, "Dad, tell us a story from your mouth!" We used to make books together too. And their inspiration is a big part of this one.

Thank you to Thomas Nunn and Adam Nunn for teaching me the fun of the story.

A big bow of gratitude to Garry Shutlak and staff members at Nova Scotia Archives and Records Management, and to the dedicated reference librarians of the Halifax Regional Library system, especially the Spring Garden Road branch. Man, are they good! Same goes to my heroes of the reference desks (including Special Collections and the University Archives) at the university libraries of Dalhousie, St. Mary's University, Mount St. Vincent University, St. Francis Xavier University (St.F.X. University Archives, too), University College of Cape Breton, Acadia University, College St. Anne, and University of King's College. I am grateful too for research assistance provided by the good folks at the Maritime Museum of the Atlantic, the Museum of Natural History, the Dartmouth Heritage Museum, and the many others at museums, big and small, in the city and throughout the province who gladly deal with my research requests no matter how offbeat they may seem at times.

A special nod to genealogy genius Terry Punch in Halifax, a co-conspirator on several of my family lineage/history stories. Terry is always graciously generous with his impressive stores of knowledge. As an expert in family trees, he's always willing to help when I find myself out on a limb.

Now that Know-It-All stories are available on screen, Wednesday night viewers of CBC TV's Canada Now program get a chance to review stories from my collection in a different way—with pictures. That work also gives me a broader view of the province. Thank you to my co-conspirator in that role, Eric Woolliscroft, producer and driver.

Did I mention I'm also available for weddings, birthdays and annual meetings? But that's another story.

Thank you to friends Nancy and John O'Donnell, the metaphysical Medici who have sustained this artist with a sponsorship greater than money, allowing him to practice his art as he may. Great computer advice too.

Finally, to the convent of Nunns from whence I hail, thank you for your interest in this on-the-air storytelling gig of mine. From the days of the Old Timer and his secretary, seems we have inherited varying degrees of 'radio' activity in our blood, so to speak. It's part of us. I hope this second published collection helps secure that part of our family heritage for you and yours to savour and to pass on.

OK, reader...Let's "Twist" again!

Enjoy!
Mr. Nova Scotia Know-It-All
Bruce Nunn 2001.

MR. NOVA SCOTIA KNOW IT ALL
— N. Bruce Nunn
2001

Fainting Goats Two: The Return!

A bizarre animal oddity comes home, 120 years later.

I met Pamela at the Christmas Parade in charming Chester Basin, on the south shore. Pamela is short and cute with a pretty face and an odd physical condition. Pamela is a goat. A goat that faints. She is one of many fainting goats all over the world that originated in Nova Scotia over a century ago.

Yeah, I know. I didn't believe it either until I saw it happen. At the starting site of the small town parade, trucks with floats attached revved their motors in the cold, morning air. There, I met Pamela the fainting goat and her cheerful owner, Debra Zong. They were getting ready.

"Yes, she's a *lot* nervous," said Debra to my first question.

My next question, obviously, was, "What happens to a fainting goat when she's nervous?"

"She stiffens up and falls over," said Debra, "in a 'faint,' as they call it."

I smirked and looked askance.

Debra smiled too but she continued. "It's called myotonia, a stiffening of the muscles almost like a muscular dystrophy," she said. "She stiffens up and falls over."

With that, my smirk exploded to convulsive laughter. Debra joined in, chuckling along, but she stuck to her story: Goats that stiffen and fall over like freshly cut Christmas trees. Timberrr!

How oddly fascinating yet strangely repulsive.

But—get this—these fainting goats were bred to do that. Long ago, goat breeders thought they could put the odd muscular condition to good use. They used the animals as scape goats. Actually they were more like bait goats.

"They were bred to put out with the sheep," said Debra.

"When the coyotes chased the sheep, the goats would faint and the coyotes would eat the goats and the sheep would get away."

These are actual goat facts. I kid you not. I've checked other sources. Debra is not making this up.

A Nova Scotian fainting goat in full flop!

Now, guess what triggers it? "A good noise and she'll go down," said Debra. "Her legs will stiffen straight and if she's moving she'll stop dead and fall over and look like a sawhorse."

Good heavens! Stiffened sawgoats!

"It's funny when you come out in the morning," said Debra who owns a small herd of these scaredy goats. "They'll do this even if they're excited or happy. You come out with your feed bucket and they're all tumbling over; this one gets the next one nervous and they're all falling over like dominoes, right?"

At this point Debra was laughing as loud as I was at the image of Pamela and her pals, like overturned coffee tables with hair.

"It's rather funny…you're trying to feed these animals upside down!"

The term 'fainting goat' is technically a misnomer. According to experts at The Atlantic Veterinary College in Charlottetown, PEI, myotonia is a naturally occurring muscular condition, a protein abnormality, triggered by being startled or excited. It just looks like fainting.

The fainting goat capital seems to be the state of Tennessee, U.S.A. Many goaters there belong to the IFGA: the International Fainting Goat Association. They have a website and everything. Check it out. Their logo is hilarious: A goat on its back, legs straight to the sky.

Oral history has it that a man named John Tinsley brought the first myotonic or fainting goats to Tennessee in the 1880s. He brought them, they say, from Nova Scotia.

In 1991, *The Economist* published the story of a Tennessee man named Mayberry who bought the first fainting goats from that Nova Scotian stranger for $36. And, a few years ago, Debra Zong bought her fainting goats in the United States and had them shipped over the border, back to their homeland, Nova Scotia. The event meant so much in fainting goat circles that it was written up in an American fainting goat newsletter called—are you ready for this?—*The Nervous News*. The fainting goats had returned to their promised land!

I thought a loud Christmas parade would be the ideal trigger for a nervous four-legged fainter. The bells, sirens, band music and cheering would surely be faint-inducing.

Parade organizer Nancy Guest was prepared with a wheelbarrow for Pamela to ride in. It wouldn't do for her to suffer a stiffening muscle spasm on foot in front of the marching team of oxen. But, miraculously, Pamela was unaffected by the din of the parade; completely faint free!

So much for my hour-long drive to witness fainting first hand.

But I wasn't giving up. I had to see this. After the parade, another hour's drive on old roads brought me to Debra Zong's animal farm in St. Croix. I was determined to see a fainting goat in full flop. She has a small herd of fainters and, sure enough, I did witness one goat fall over, legs outstretched, muscles tightened, sawhorse style. Amazing!

It lasted about ten seconds, then the goat was up and gambolling gaily again. They do exist! Yes, Virginia, there is a fainting goat. And Debra Zong's little bleaters are official, original, repatriated, Nova Scotian fainting goats!

Surgeons Underground!

*A new piece of Springhill's mine rescue story:
Halifax doctors down in the deeps.*

We think of sterile hands and clean white masks when we think of surgeons. Can you picture a surgeon in a dusty black coal mine? Neither could they until it happened unexpectedly during a mine rescue drama in Springhill, Nova Scotia. I thought documentary makers and writers had exhausted all there was to say about the town's mine disaster history until I happened upon this piece of the drama, never before told publicly.

After six days buried alive, twelve Springhill miners were rescued in the fall of 1958. Then word came there were seven more men trapped thirteen thousand feet underground. No food, no water, no light. The world was soon aware of this Nova Scotian mine disaster. And some young surgeons at the Victoria General Hospital in Halifax decided to go to Springhill to help. But they ended up way out of their element.

Drs. Charles Graham and Garth Vaughan remember it. Both retired, they agreed to reunite and tell me their story.

In the middle of the night, they rode in two ambulances with a pile of drugs and medical supplies donated by the V.G. The ambulances raced over Halifax Harbour to Shearwater airbase where the surgeons boarded a clanky military helicopter. It was cold and noisy as they flew low over Fundy Bay, narrowly skirting high-tension wires as the chopper landed on a well-lit baseball field in the mining town.

"There were lights, cars all lined up," said Dr. Vaughan. "The RCMP had arranged it."

Cars from all over town "just parked in a big circle around the ball field and shone their lights into the pitcher's area," he said. "You couldn't miss that as we came over Springhill!"

The surgeons helped treat injured miners in Springhill's hospital.

During a break, they ventured over to the mine's crowded pithead where weeping relatives were holding a nervous vigil for miners still trapped far below. The young doctors just wanted to see what was happening. They casually joined the crowd, watching and waiting. At that moment, unexpectedly, a rescue worker appeared at the mouth of the mine saying they found the second group of trapped men and needed doctors down there.

Everyone knew who these out-of-towners were standing behind the rope near the mine entrance. So, even though they had never been down a mine, the visiting doctors felt compelled to step forward. They did so nervously.

Their long trip down into the deeps in a rattling mining car on rails has marked their memories for life. "It made quite a noise, there's a rumble," said Dr. Graham.

"There was water dripping down overhead and it was cold; it was really eerie," said Dr. Vaughan. "The only light was flashing around from these headlamps that we had on."

Dr. Graham admired the courage shown by the draegermen—the rescuers—and by the other miners. "This was totally strange to me," he said, "and I was afraid."

Dr. Charles Graham of Halifax treated Springhill miners trapped underground.

In that dark, small, foreign space underground, the medical men were as far removed from the order and brightness of an operating room as they could possibly imagine. But they were there and they were needed. They felt they had to do whatever they could.

"I was only 30 at the time," said Dr. Vaughan. "We knew the miners down there were about our ages and had families at home waiting for them."

The mining car's wheels kept rolling down deeper and deeper into the black, dank pit. "When we got to the bottom and got out of this car they started to lead us through this tunnel they had dug through to these people," said Dr. Vaughan. "It wasn't very big; it was a crawl space."

Then came the job of removing the suffering, malnourished miners from the underground cell that had held them prisoner for over a week.

The rescuers weren't sure what kind of condition the men would be in. They told the doctors, "either they're going to crawl out past or we're going to bring them out on stretchers," said Dr. Vaughan.

As the men were brought out of the tunnel, the doctors treated them

Dr. Garth Vaughan of Windsor entered the deeps for the first time.

with cannisters of oxygen and water. They immobilized fractured legs and arms to make the rough trip up the slope less painful.

Once on the surface, the injured miners were taken to the local hospital where the town's surgeon, Dr. Carson Murray—singer Anne Murray's father—was glad to have help from the Halifax doctors.

The doctors did cut downs on their blackened, sooty patients, cutting swollen, injured and burned flesh to reach a vein and insert intravenous lines carrying fluid.

Some miners went by land ambulance to the Victoria General in Halifax where Drs. Graham and Vaughan also returned.

The 'bump' of '58 claimed seventy-five miners' lives. But these city surgeons saw the Springhill miracle happen: a second group of men, given up for dead by some, had escaped their grave, far underground, down in the dark of the Cumberland mine.

Amherst's Big Booze Heist!

'Upstanding' merchants rob
Parrsboro of illegal rum stash.

This story about booze is a double shot. Part One packs a punch but it's followed by a Part Two chaser, which freshens the story with more details, details that flowed from Nova Scotian listeners after the first part was poured onto the CBC Radio airwaves. I love when that happens in this radio storytelling business: my telling of the story becomes part of the story. Enjoy.

R um! Big sloshing barrels full of it. Enough to get a herd of elephants drunk. That's how much illegal liquor was stolen in the great prohibition booze heist in Parrsboro in 1925. Rum running and bootlegging spilled over everywhere back then; Amherst was soaked in it. It was a gang of Amherst merchants who planned the Parrsboro heist like an Al Capone caper. But it all ended in scandal.

Harry Block was there. At 87, the Amherst native remembers the illegal escapade in some detail. His father drove one of the getaway trucks that night.

"My father called me in and asked me to take the licence plates off the truck and put the tarpaulin in and go up to the garage and fill the truck up with gasoline," said Harry as we talked at his Halifax home. A boy of eleven at the time, Harry felt the excitement. He knew something was up and wanted to be part of it. So he hid in the back of his dad's black Model-T truck, under the tarp.

But he was discovered and sent back into the house to bed. His father, Israel Block, left their Acadia Street home that night and drove the old gravel road down to Parrsboro with several other vehicles. The plan was to hold up the big brick Customs House where rum kegs and whiskey seized from a vessel in the Fundy Bay were locked up.

The Amherst gang was made up not of mobsters, but of merchants: a bank manager, a funeral parlour owner, a garage mechanic, and many others.

"They were all fine businessmen but they decided to take the law into their own hands and heist the booze," said Harry, quite matter-of-factly, grinning.

Running illegal alcohol was a commonplace, risky, but entertaining venture then. For these upstanding Amherst folk, it was a fun and lucrative crime. Harry is quite amused by it all, even now.

They were serious about getting the hooch though. There was great strength in their numbers. The *Amherst Daily News* of May 20, 1926 reported, "There were between 25 and 30 others who were gathered at the rendezvous in Parrsboro, the night of the raid."

Al Capone would have loved that kind of backup.

First, someone in the gang cut the phone wire to the Customs House.

Uh-Oh. While cutting, something went wrong. "It gave off one sound, one signal," said Harry, "that I suppose awakened the town or the customs officers."

Harry Block, whose father drove the getaway car in the Amherst booze heist.

Despite that mistake, many kegs of rum and boxes of whiskey were quickly taken from the customs house by truck. Even the daughter of the Amherst funeral parlour owner heaved some hooch into the hearse! Talk about dying for a drink!

"It became kind of a joke among the businessmen," said Harry, "there was quite a laugh among them all!"

But Harry's dad wasn't laughing all the way home. He barely made it back to his house. As he drove into Amherst, his Model-T, laden with 12 heavy wooden rum kegs, he saw a cop on the corner. But the policeman was part of the gang so he waved Harry through. A few blocks later, a cop not in on the caper fired shots at the speeding truck, taking out a tire!

Despite the shot-up tire, Israel Block "kept on going until he got home and unloaded the booze." Safe!

He hid the barrels in his barn beside his house. Harry remembers, as a boy, looking out very early the next morning. Steam was shooting from the old truck's taxed engine and his father was changing the tire. He knew something big had happened.

But it wasn't a clean getaway for all.

Harry recalls that a garage mechanic who drove one of the getaway trucks was caught and gave up some names. Yet, in the end, only five men were charged. Their names were listed in the newspaper of the day: a Mr. P.K. Atkinson, Mr. G. Blanche and a Mr. McKim all pleaded guilty to receiving stolen liquor. A Mr. Coates and Mr. Fife admitted to the stealing.

Obviously many accomplices got away.

Each of the five was fined a whopping $1,000 and handed a token ten days in jail. As Harry recalls, the lenient jail sentence was treated just like the rum robbery itself—as a bit of a lark.

"They were only sentenced during the day," he said. "At nighttime, the jailer and the gang got together and were driving around town!"

Drinking rum, no doubt.

The stolen kegs were never recovered by police. Harry thinks the spirits were spirited away by the Amherst gang, over the border, out of the province.

Ahhh, here's to the grand old era of prohibition in Nova Scotia: Cheers!

Now, that's the gist of the great rum robbery story of 1925 that I told on CBC Radio's "Information Morning" in Nova Scotia. Then my phone started ringing. More people wanted to add their rum heist anecdotes, in intoxicating detail. One caller even tipped me to the identity of that arrested mechanic who had squealed on the others. THAT was interesting. Here's Amherst's Big Booze Heist, Part Two.

Here's a new twist to that rum robbery adventure. Hmmm, rum with a twist. Sounds good doesn't it? Well it seems that Amherst-to-Parrsboro run for the rum had more twists than I realized. There's new information.

Remember, a 1926 *Amherst Daily News* article confirmed for me that almost thirty rum robbers were in on the Parrsboro raid. One of them had goofed and accidentally alerted the customs inspector. How? Well, that's where a new source with an old memory comes in. He is Murdock Rodger, known as "Dock", an 81-year-old retired car dealership owner in Amherst. I talked to him after I had told Part One of this story.

Dock told me that the mob of merchants not only broke into the building, "they also broke open a couple of kegs of booze and were making so much noise they woke the customs inspector up!"

So, tipping off the authorities didn't come from cutting the phone line. It was the thieves getting tipsy that did the tipping! They just couldn't wait to wet their whistles. Then all Heck broke loose.

"They all took off with the inspector in pursuit!"

The car chase was on! Picture Al Capone and the Keystone Cops. That was the scene: about thirty rum robbers in a fleet of Model-T's, all laden with sloshing rum kegs. One robber drove a speeding hearse— bearing heavy casks, not caskets. The line of black trucks snaked through the night on the windy gravel road back to Amherst.

Even Halifax lawyer Clare Christie, an Amherstonian by birth, recalls her father retelling this tale. Just like in the movies, when the pursuing inspector moved in, hot on the bumper, "they rolled the barrels of rum off the back of the truck," she said, "into (his) vehicle."

Docky Rodger remembers that the fleeing robbers also tried to lose their tail by splitting up at a fork in the road. The pursuing inspector "couldn't go both ways so he went after the fellas that went Springhill way; one of them was Edgar Cole."

And Edgar Cole, the Amherst mechanic, was caught!

At this point in the story, there's a modern-day twist. A caller phoned to tell me that mechanic was kin to a currently sitting Provincial Judge in Amherst. I gasped for air. You see, I'm allergic to libeling the family of someone who can put me in jail.

But Judge David E. Cole heard my story and called me up, amused. This distinguished member of the judiciary, a lifelong Amherst resident, had never heard that he might be linked to such notorious illegality. So he did some checking of his own. In fact it was him who put me on to good old Dock Rodger. Judge Cole took the facts of the story as I had told it, and went to ask Docky what he knew about it. Could this be true?

"Well," said the judge, "I got about three words out so he knew what I was talking about and I mentioned the driver of one of the vehicles and he started to laugh. He said, 'that was your father!'"

The judge was bemused and befuddled to learn about a side of his dad he had never known. I'm thankful for a mirthful magistrate. However, I then had to broach the subject of how the police had tracked down the rum gang's leaders. It would appear the judge's dad gave them up! He was a snitch!

"I guess he must have been just trying to do his civic duty," the judge joked.

Or maybe he offered the names to buy his own freedom. "I did note that he wasn't named among those that got charged," said the judge. Perhaps he was the "one who ratted." Note, it was not me who used the word "ratted."

Rat or not, Edgar Cole was simply living life to the fullest as a young, single man in prohibition Amherst.

As for the numerous kegs of stolen hooch, Docky Rodger thinks the booze had been bound for these Amherst rumrunners in the first place, right off the boat. He figures they had actually stolen back their own illegal goods. And the cops never retrieved it.

SENTENCES IMPOSED ON AMHERST MEN

Five Amherstonians fined for part in Parrsboro affair.

ALL RECEIVE JAIL TERMS

Judge Patterson delivers strong reprimand to accused men.

The much discussed Parrsboro liquor raid was brought to a speedy conclusion this morning, when Percy Atkinson, G. F. Blanche, E. F. McKim, Roy Coates and Lloyd Fife, appeared before Judge Patterson in the County Court, and pleaded guilty to individual charges. After a particularly strong reprimand had been delivered by Judge Patterson each man was fined one thousand dollars, with a jail sentence of ten days. In default of payment within the next ten days, the Judge stated that a ten month sentence would be served.

Expected sensations in this case failed to materialize when the Atkinson, Blanche and McKim charged with receiving, stole liquor, while Messrs Coates and Fife were charged with the theft of liquors from the Customs House, Parrsboro.

James A. Hanway, K.C. who acted as counsel for the accused, entered a plea to Judge Patterson's leniency. F. L. Milner, K.C., Prosecutor for Cumberland, presented a full resume of his address, urged the presiding Judge devise the punishment.

In delivering his charge, Judge Patterson reviewed the various points in the case, and attached some significance to the fact that the five men were involved in the activities in the Customs House. He referred to the fact that between twenty-five and twenty-five who were gathered in Parrsboro for the raid. With other men involved, brought into the light, and pronounced into custody, heavy fines.

Cecil Langille, with assault of employee of the Foundry Co., was given a twenty day sentence in the County jail and two hundred dollars fine for the peace.

As for...

Harry Block thought his father's truck full of rum kegs was eventually spirited out of the province. Docky recalls a lot of the rum was left hidden in those old barns throughout the Tantramar region until it was forgotten.

"It was discovered off and on for a period of years before it was all cleaned up!"

There you have it, a double rum story with a twist; here's to your health!

Clara and The Duke

The hunt for an Ellington jazz tune named for a Nova Scotian.

This, I think, was my finest hour in my years of CBC Know-It-Allism; an investigative adventure with all the right elements: A remarkable, meaningful, Nova Scotian story, a burst of frantic phoning, a few flukes, some family ties, and in the process, unwittingly becoming a part of the story myself! And it was a world exclusive! It doesn't get any better than this.

It began with a special international anniversary that I thought could be tied in with a local angle. Duke Ellington—once called the greatest jazz musician that ever lived, a musical genius, at the forefront of the exciting Cotton Club jazz scene in New York—was being honoured.

On the one hundredth anniversary of his birth, April 29, 1999, celebrations and tributes to his music were happening everywhere, in over three dozen cities. On a less grand level, it was also a day of special, personal meaning for a woman in Nova Scotia, a relative of the Dixon family of Halifax.

The Dixons' roots stretch back to historic Africville, the closely-knit community of Black families that once thrived on the edge of Bedford Basin at the north end of the Halifax peninsula. It's gone now, replaced by modern urban parkland. But it was once a place of warm, wonderful folks, tight ties with church and neighbours, and late-night jamming sessions of the best music you'd ever want to hear.

The Dixons were proud to claim the famous jazz master Duke Ellington as family. When he and his jazz band came to Halifax to play gigs during the 1950s and 1960s, The Duke himself would drop in on the Dixon household on Forrester Street, 'round the turn,' as they called it, around the curve of the traintracks from the heart of Africville. Then he'd amble down the street to visit Newlie (Florence (Dixon) David) another Dixon relative. Everybody loved to hang out at Newlie's, playing music and having parties.

Dr. Ruth Johnson, a former resident and now historian of Africville, told me Duke used to give out free tickets to his evening performance.

The book *Africville: A Spirit Lives On* shows a photograph of the legendary Ellington sitting, smiling broadly, with train porter George Dixon and Africville teacher Gordon Jemmott on the living room sofa at the Dixons' house. It's a small faded bit of proof that this great

Jazz great Duke Ellington (centre) hanging out at the Dixons' home in Halifax.

man of music did indeed hang out with these lucky folks, his Halifax family. It was a home away from home for one of the century's greatest musicians, living on the road.

That precious photo came from Stella (Dixon) Carvery. Her daughter is Clara (Carvery) Adams. Clara, now 60, still lives 'round the turn' where the former Africville site once was. It's now a city park next to an industrial shipping container pier. The week of the big Ellington anniversary, I visited Clara at her home in that end of town to ask

Clara (Carvery) Adams and husband, Bucky: thrilled to hear her lost Ellington song for the first time.

about her memories of the jazz legend, Duke Ellington.

"Whenever he came to Nova Scotia he would come to visit the family; Stella and Reggie, my parents," she said. "I remember him being in the kitchen. I remember him going through the house just like an everyday person because he was family."

She was simply and casually acknowledging a favorite family memory. "Not just because he was Duke Ellington, he didn't make us feel that he was, you know…(special) because he was The Duke," she said. "He would come and make us feel like he was part of the family, which he was."

They liked having him around and he liked being with them. So what is the connection that made Duke Ellington feel like family to Clara? It's an amazing story.

The night Ellington opened at New York's high-class Cotton Club in the late 1920s, he met and immediately fell for Mildred Dixon. She was a beautiful New York dancer whose family came from Africville in Halifax but had moved down to Boston. Striking out on her own, Mildred later went to the Big Apple where she and a Henri Wesson danced in a duo billed "Mildred and Henri," one of the finest "ballroom" dance acts in the United States at the time.

Mercer Ellington, Duke's son, described Mildred Dixon in his biography of his father: "Mil was petite, with long black hair swept back into a bun, ballerina style. Her finely chiseled features and luminous dark eyes somehow suggested the East Indies."

No wonder Ellington was drawn to her. He and Mildred quickly paired up and were together throughout the 1930s and remained close through life. Mildred became a mother to Mercer Ellington, a son from Duke's previous and only marriage.

"She had innate class comparable to Ellington's own," writes Mercer Ellington, "and he showed her great courtesy, attention, and affection."

"Her devotion was obvious, and they made a graceful pair. She was intelligent and had a gift for diplomacy that made for friends in every quarter. She was popular with those he dealt with in the business and was trusted."

It seems the dancer with Africville roots helped Ellington both personally and professionally in those early days. She accompanied Ellington with the band when they went on tour. Mercer has nothing but praise for her. "Mil always carried herself like the lady she genuinely was," he writes, "and in time she gained everyone's confidence. She was a real asset to Pop, his 'Sweet Bebe.'"

According to Mercer Ellington, his father and Mildred Dixon were "deeply involved."

Even later in their careers, after they parted company, Ellington looked after Mildred Dixon when she injured her back and could no longer dance.

Clara, in Halifax, put me in touch with her aunt, Vivian (Dixon) Maxwell, Mildred's first cousin. Also an Africville native who moved to New York, Vivian told me over the long distance line that she worked the concession stands at the city's night clubs and used to hang out with Duke and Mildred. She recalls Mildred was a talented performer in her own right.

"She was a chorus dancer," said Vivian. "She worked in Europe and France. She worked in New York and years ago at the Cotton Club."

That was before she teamed up with Ellington. And afterwards, once injured, she had no way of supporting herself. So, with The Duke's help, Mildred went into business.

"That's when she stopped dancing," said Vivian from New York. "She had a talent agency. He owned the agency that she ran."

And many years later, after Mildred died, Ellington continued to visit her relatives in Halifax whenever he blew into town with his band.

So, yes, to Clara Carvery Adams and her parents and her mother's

family, the Dixons, including her grandfather George Dixon in that
photo, Duke Ellington was family in the best sense.

That's why Clara holds dear memories of Duke Ellington jamming
at her next-door neighbour's house with anyone who stopped by.
"Whatever they played that night at a dance…bongos, whatever it took
to make music, they were there and the show went on and Duke
Ellington would jam with the bunch," she said.

I asked her what that was like, having this great icon of jazz sophisti-
cation, this famous fellow Black person, linked with her family and
jamming with her people, sharing that bond of music and background
right there in her own neighbourhood.

She smiled. "As an experience, it was great. It was beautiful to have
The Duke sit in with just locals and play…he did!"

Better than that, Clara even got a chance to meet The Duke on his
own turf, in New York City. She was visiting Mildred, her mother's
cousin. She found herself in a big, fancy house at 815 Riverside Drive.

"I was just a little girl but I remember going into this huge home and
taking an elevator and going up to maybe two or three floors in that
household. It was beautiful."

"Who was there?" I asked.

"Mildred was there, Mercer, a little girl who I think was Mercer's
daughter, and Duke Ellington," said Clara.

"You remember seeing him in New York," I asked stupidly, a little
dumbfounded.

"Oh my goodness yes, I sure do! He was a beautiful person."

My conversation with Clara was enjoyable and enlightening. I was
learning about a section of Nova Scotian Black heritage I had only
heard of in casual mentions. It was more like urban myth that the great
Duke Ellington was somehow linked to local folks, that he played here a
few times. Well, now I knew it was true. I had the details. A great story
in itself. But as we wrapped up our chat, Clara floored me with this
story:

"I think the last time I was in Duke's company," she said, "was when he
was staying at the Citadel Inn, here in Halifax; can't remember the year."

She thinks it was sometime in the 1950s when she was a young woman, before she was married. "My mother, Stella Carvery, and I had gone in to see him at the hotel room because he was performing that night, I think at The Lobstertrap," she said.

"That's when he said to me, 'I'm going to write a song,' you know…about me!"

My eyes opened wider. Duke Ellington promised a song to her?

"He says, 'I'm going to name it 'Clara,'" said Clara.

I blinked in disbelief. This was big. Did she have the song? What did it sound like? Where was it? Clara couldn't tell me. She had never heard it. She didn't know if Ellington had fulfilled his promise or not. She had heard that he had begun the tune but died (in 1974), leaving it unfinished. She felt she'd never really know the truth. Perhaps the tune penned in her name never existed. Her husband, a musician, had been curious about it for years, too. She'd often told friends in the Black community about The Duke's musical promise to her. But with no verification, perhaps it was just one of those lines a worldly star of the stage feeds a pretty young woman just to see the sparkle in her eyes. Duke Ellington wrote a song for YOU? You might not blame folks for being skeptical of Clara's claim.

It was a long shot but I decided to try to find the song. I did what I do in these cases. I started cold calling everyone with any connection to the topic—in this case, experts in the jazz world. Andrew Homzy of Concordia University was a recognized Ellingtonian I read about in that week's newspaper coverage of all the Ellington tribute concerts. Homzy spent a year searching the Ellington archives in Washington and London, where thousands of compositions, long and short, bright and dark, are mined constantly by jazz aficionados. Homzy told me he had never heard of a tune called "Clara" but he promised to check into it for me after the centenary hoopla subsided.

OK. So, I waited. And while I waited I made more calls. There were few Ellington experts who were safe from my research. From Montreal to New York to Washington, I jumped into the upper jazz echelons: Verve Records, New York's Jazz Ellington Centre, the owners of Tempo records and Famous Music—even the famous Oscar Brandt, then of the Museum of American Music in New York. He agreed to call around his circles and he actually phoned me back! Seems, no one he knew had ever heard of an Ellington tune entitled "Clara."

But after all that fruitless phoning, a package arrived in the mail. It was from the National Museum of American History, part of the Smithsonian Institution in Washington. It was such a busy time in Ellington circles, my calls to that collection didn't get very far. But Ellington expert Andrew Homzy's request on my behalf apparently got swifter attention. The request had been answered. When I pulled out pages of sheet music, my jaw dropped. There it was. A complete copy of the music for a full instrumental jazz orchestra piece: piano, sax, trombone, horns, the works! And written right across the top, it said "Clara." That was it! Pages and pages of musical notes scratched in black ink on the lined scoresheets and signed at the bottom. I was holding Ellington's composition for Clara!

The archivist at the Smithsonian wrote to me that the song had never been published, never recorded and, just as Clara Carvery Adams had heard, never even completed. As far as the archivist knew, the world had never heard it. It wasn't listed on any Ellington discographies in that collection, which is why it took a while for the archivist to find "Clara." She also pointed out that it had never been copyrighted and was in the public domain.

No one had really known about the tune except Ellington, Clara, and her relatives. Here was a memorable slice of her family history and an important musical piece of Nova Scotian Black heritage. So, what to do with it?

Obviously the only way to tell this part of the story was to hear the composition; if not in full orchestra, then at least in a simpler rendition. The CBC's master of things musical in Halifax, Glenn Meisner, recognized the historical and cultural importance of this jazzy find and agreed to have it recorded. He and the technically talented recording wiz Karl Falkenham joined me in a conspiratorial surprise for the song's namesake. This was going to be great. Arrangements were made to summon two musicians.

Up in Studio H on the top floor of the CBC Radio building, where most Maritime music greats have recorded, piano player Bill Stevenson sat at the keyboard. And on the saxophone—get this—was Clara's husband, Bucky Adams, a veteran sax player in Halifax music circles. He had been curious about this tune for years. He had told me he would love to be able to get this music, to play it for his wife Clara, for whom it was named.

Then it was time for the sting. I sent a cab across town for Clara. Unsure what I or her husband Bucky was up to, she arrived. Up the elevator to the top floor, looking a little confused, Clara said hello. I escorted her into the big studio control room where we both sat to take in the recording session. Through the wide studio glass, we watched. Sitting there, Clara listened to what she had waited to hear for over forty years: her Duke Ellington song called "Clara" being played for the first time in decades—with her husband Bucky performing it on sax.

I handed Clara the Ellington music sheets, as she reacted to the rich, easy, beautiful, sax instrumental pouring through the big studio speakers.

It was a truly magical moment.

Softly, she said, "Reality has set in." Then a little giggle. The music wafted loudly over us.

"…To hear it," she said. Then a pause. The raspy, robust sax vibrating wonderfully in our ears.

"That's his own handwriting you're looking at," I said.

"Is it really," she gasped. "I'm devastated. I'm overwhelmed. I can't believe it. Is it really?"

More music, rising and falling in lovely, warm tones, a jazz instrumental ballad, not just heard but felt through tingles in the skin.

"Ohhhh," she sighed. She was speechless. The papers in her hand trembled.

"That's his signature," I said. "There's your name right across the top."

"Right across the board, right across the top, that's me!"

Clara was smiling, her eyes tearing up. She spoke in emotional fragments.

"What a feeling…I can't believe…I knew it was there somewhere…had to be…he was a man of his word…I knew it had to be somewhere…this is the first time I've seen the music and heard the song…now I know…reality has…"

She couldn't finish her thought. It was really hitting home for her. This was what she had waited for most of her life. Her husband too.

"You know it was so important to Bucky to get this done but I didn't realize how important…you know, Duke Ellington made a song…!"

I think she wanted to add "for ME!"

"I can't believe it," she repeated as the music swelled.

With satisfied sighs, Clara slowly shook her head in wonder as she glanced over the pages of handwritten musical notes, pages she never dreamed she would ever see. The music flowed from overhead and Clara absorbed it, deeply touched, and thoroughly taken aback.

The Movie Mogul from Mulgrave

From the Canso Causeway to Charlie Chaplin.

You do this Nova Scotia Know-It-All gig long enough and you begin to think there was one of 'us' in on just about every major starting point and turning point in modern world history. Strange as it sounds, I'm becoming increasingly convinced that the trade winds of time and chance have blown us Bluenoses into just about every interesting nook and corner of significant change around the globe. It doesn't even surprise me anymore! I didn't even blink when I learned that Charlie Chaplin and the Keystone Cops, icons of the very beginning of feature film making, were touched by the talent of an energetic lad from rural Nova Scotia. Of course they were!

His filmography lists over two hundred motion pictures—some big time films, some 'B' movies—which he acted in or produced. Born May 5, 1891, in Guysborough County, Wallace Archibald MacDonald had a long career of Hollywood hustle. He was our movie mogul from Mulgrave!

Fellow Hollywood producer Dan Petrie from Glace Bay remembers this early movie maker. Dan returned my call from Toronto where, amazingly, at 79, he was making yet another movie for the entertainment industry which he also conquered south of the border.

"We knew in Nova Scotia that Wallace was from our part of the world," said Dan. "He was kind of a middling star."

Wallace MacDonald appeared in seven Charlie Chaplin flicks, including the very first ones in 1914: *Caught in a Cabaret, Mabel's Married Life, Face on the Bar Room Floor* and the first feature length comedy ever made, *Tillie's Punctured Romance,* in which he played one of the classic Keystone Cops. This Bluenose lad was a genuine pioneer in film.

So, how did he get from Mulgrave to movieland?

Colin Purcell, an amateur collector of Mulgrave history, told me he grew up hearing about this famous fellow, Wallace MacDonald. He learned that Wallace MacDonald got his first name from his mother Clara Wallace, of the well-to-do Mulgrave merchant family. Colin told me Wallace's family left Mulgrave when he was young.

"They moved to Sydney around 1900," said Colin. "And some time after that he got involved in this film in Hollywood."

His mother was a talented piano player who taught Wallace to play and may have encouraged some dramatic acting out in skits about the house.

He began working at age 12 as an errand boy at Sydney's Dosco Steel Company. By about age 17 Wallace was a junior clerk with the Royal Bank in Sydney. But soon he was going down the road, out to western Canada.

Alan H. MacDonald, a nephew of the movie man, told me in a letter from Australia that Wallace had joined some travelling theatre companies, ending up on the American southwest circuit. His mother ended up in that region too, briefly.

Wallace MacDonald's Hollywood star shone quite brightly.

In the 1920s the fan magazines voted this Nova Scotian, "the most handsome leading man in Hollywood."(That according to one-time *Halifax Herald* writer Alex Nickerson).

The 1918 Sydney newspaper quotes *Motion Picture Classic Magazine,*

Hollywood movie man Wallace
MacDonald, right; father Archibald,
centre; brother Vincent, left.

which called Wallace MacDonald
the new "King of Charm in
Hollywood."

He had the looks.

Throughout the 1920s, "he
participated in many successful
features," writes Alan H.
MacDonald, "including *Blockade,
Drums of the Desert, Love and
Glory, Madame Sphinx, Maytime,
The Sea Hawk, The Spoilers,
Spotlight Sadie,* and *The Fighting
Shepherdess.*"

MacDonald produced Rita
Hayworth's first picture with
Columbia pictures. You know
what? I think I should say that
again: A guy from Mulgrave
produced Rita Hayworth's first
film! Our infiltration into world events couldn't get any more subversive.
It's as if we, as a province, planned all this. The Bluenose Conspiracy. The
odd thing is, it seems these twists and links just seem to 'happen' with us.

Our Mulgrave movieman also produced a few Boris Carloff features.
MacDonald's many westerns included titles such as *Gunmen from Laredo
and Phantom Stagecoach.* He appeared as hero, sidekick and villain and
was even billed higher than a young newcomer named John Wayne.

In the early 1930s, MacDonald turned from acting to producing. His
last on-screen role was in the final scenes of *Flying Down to Rio* with
Fred Astaire.

A very prolific performer!

But before all this success, Wallace MacDonald's new career was put on
hold for World War One. He left silent film making temporarily, returned
to Nova Scotia, and joined the 10th Siege Battery, part of the Royal Canadian Artillery and was stationed at York Redoubt, near Halifax.

Post war, he returned to movie making. Here's a neat discovery: he appeared in a movie called *Gold Diggers of 1933* in which the star was a huge Hollywood name, Ruby Keeler, from Dartmouth. I wonder if they knew of their shared heritage?

Like Ruby Keeler (and like Dan Petrie for that matter), Wallace MacDonald kept in touch with his roots. He wrote many letters home to family. He also came back briefly to write and act in a movie-making company based in Cape Breton in the 1920s.

But by 1959, after 45 years in the industry, he retired to Camarillo, California with his wife, Helen Lee, an actress who appeared under the name Doris May. He died at age 87 in 1978 and is buried with his wife in California.

Addendum: This was one of the first stories I had researched in which I did not rely on the usual convoluted, twisted chain of investigative, round-the-globe phone calls. Forgive me, I used the internet. I didn't want to. To fact finders like me, it felt wrong. As if it were replacing the instincts and 'phone skills' and helpful coincidental encounters that go along with traditional investigative information gathering by phone. The phone is the journalist's friend. The internet is like his drive-through bank machine, dispensing facts instead of cash at his finger-tips. Too quick. Too easy. Too impersonal. Where's the charm? The people factor? The fascinating folks you meet amid the chase?

Well, let me tell you, through some sort of twist, the people won out in this story hunt.

Sure, the computer filled some big gaps in my search for Wallace MacDonald: I found his complete filmography on the net. I even saw a photo of his final resting place via this little cyber secret which I will share with only you: findagrave.com. Bizarre proof you can indeed find anything on earth or under it on the world wide web.

But I was most heartened when I received a key reply to my many web searches and e-mailings. It was a phone call from Wallace MacDonald's former next door neighbours in Camarillo, California. It seems someone, somewhere, had decided to print my electronic e-mail inquiry in the old fashioned medium, the community newspaper; in this case it was the *Ventura County Star* in California.

I was able to tell Anne Erspamer and the other neighbours much more about their famous friend's background than a humble Wallace MacDonald had ever let on. Also from California, Ray and Sandy Clancy wrote me. Their family history research shows they are relatives of the Clancy's, who were Nova Scotian neighbours of Wallace MacDonald in Mulgrave. They have old photos to prove it.

A good old-fashioned letter to the editor and a couple of personal, voice-to-voice telephone conversations: That's what clinched this story for me.

Ropin' and Ridin' on Sable Island

How children's protests saved Sable's horsey history.

John Diefenbaker and the Sable Island horses—a Canadian Country band? Well, actually it's more of a headline for a unique historical event about forty years ago when politics and ponies crossed paths.

Contrary to folklore that has Sable's first horses as survivors of a shipwreck, the fact is they were intentionally shipped there in 1737. A Boston clergyman thought it a fine place to let horses graze. Lots of open land, good grass, away from thieves, and no fences required. But most of that first herd died. In 1760 more horses were shipped out by a Boston merchant who had taken most of his horses from expelled Acadians. During the next century, stallions were sent out to breed with the Sable horses. (And yes, they are actually horses, not ponies.)

Historians at The Maritime Museum of the Atlantic have told me that, as late as 1940, Sable horses were still being rounded up and sold in Halifax for low prices. There was still no special protection for them, even into the 1950s. That's why people living on Sable manning the island's weather station could use the horses for hauling heavy supplies and for riding around the island.

When Arthur Dooks was the superintendent on the island in the 1950s, his wife, Audrey, was mother and school teacher to their children. She remembers the men ropin' and ridin' on Sable Island. "They had corrals. They would round them up and break them in bit by bit," she told me when I called her at her home in Head of Jeddore.

They used heavy sand bags on the horses at first, to get them used to human weight. Audrey told me even she rode an island horse. And at low tide, the island workers held horse races on the beach.

In May 1960, all that changed. The federal government's Crown Assets Disposal Corporation offered all the Sable Island horses for sale.

They wrongly thought the horses were stunted due to inbreeding and little food. Hay drops from airplanes were largely ignored by the horses, used to eating the beach grass in the sandy dunes. They were living a natural, wild existence during good times and difficult times. They were simply surviving and succumbing in the harsh but normal circle of life. Yet, the horses were to be sold off the island, likely to be turned into dog food.

Many Canadian schoolchildren wrote to Prime Minister Diefenbaker asking that the horses remain on their island, free from human intervention.

Sable Islanders once saddled and rode these wild island horses.

The Dief responded positively. It became law under part of the Canadian Shipping Act that no person shall feed or have anything to do with the horses without written permission. They were left to roam free and survive or perish, as true wild animals.

But in 1964 some workers on Sable were tempted to intervene when disease struck the horse population. About half of the horses perished. Norman Bell of Orangedale Cape Breton lived on Sable with his wife during the 1960s, maintaining the power plant. The sad sight of some sick horses, motionless with heads hanging, moved him.

"In a few hours they would've been down," he told me in a craggy, caring voice touched with a wee lilt, discernable even on the long distance line. "Would we wait for them to die or shoot them," he asked hypothetically.

They never fired a shot. Or learned what the disease was. Many horses died. The Bells grew close to one group, giving them pet names, including a mare they called Topsy. But, heartbroken, they had to watch their four-legged friends perish—even a pretty colt with his head hanging heavily that they noticed. Mr. Bell ran for some brown sugar, held the colt's mouth open and tried to force it to eat.

"It just stood there," he said sadly. "By morning they were all dead. It was a sad thing but it wasn't well known."

Summer was happier on the island. When the herd was healthy, they were a marvel to behold. Wild horses running freely across the wind-swept sand dunes just outside the Bells' kitchen window were a common occurrence.

"You'd see them just tripping over the dunes, one after the other," said Mr. Bell. "Oh, we had nice photographs."

Dashing stallions and mares with offspring lagging behind; a daily miracle of nature swooshing through his backyard! Living, struggling, surviving and dying together. They were the Bells' good neighbours, their close friends.

"Ohhhh yes!" His voice was happy now with the memory.

"To us the horses were part of the community," said Mr. Bell. "You might say they were part of us at the time."

Rising Tide Rescue

A family fighting Fundy's tide
pin their last hope on one man.

This terrifying true story is every parent's nightmare.

In 1948, a young girl and boy, aged eleven and ten, were fishing alone out on the far point of a rocky shoal. They didn't notice the deceiving Fundy Bay tides rising quickly behind them. Soon, deep water surrounded the shoal. It was April and cold. A wide, icy, watery gap expanded by the minute, separating the kids from safe shore.

The water rose rapidly. Even the spot where they stood would soon be swallowed up by the world's highest tides.

Ruby White and her younger brother Junior grew up there at Lower Cove in Chignecto Bay, a finger of Fundy, in Cumberland County.

Ruby lives in Alberta now; Junior is in Ontario. They remember their fear that day, 53 years ago, as if it were yesterday. In a telephone conference call I arranged, they told me what happened.

"I was fishin'," said Junior, "and told Ruby to go look where the gap was and she said 'come on we gotta go' and I said 'let me catch one more'. It was too late then."

"That was really scary," said Ruby. "The water started comin' in, but we never noticed!"

They had no choice but to wade through the water-filled gap, trying to step on invisible underwater rocks.

"We tried to walk but I just about went over my head when I got off the reef," said Ruby.

They were stranded, wet, cold, and hollering for help from the rocky 'reef,' as they called it. The water kept rising.

Earl Bourgeois responded first, plunging his horse-pulled coal cart into the water. But a wheel got stuck on an underwater rock. As the tide hit the horse's nose, the animal panicked and surged back to the beach.

Then the kids' older brother Danny White, aged fifteen, flew into action. "I ran down and I jumped in the water and tried to swim out to them but I took cramps," he said from his home in River Hebert.

The frigid water was unbearable. The little ones moved up to the top of the shoal. The unforgiving Fundy tide continued quickly creeping up.

Word got to the children's father, Placide White, a coal miner who showed up fast and rushed into the water, on horseback. He got to the rocky shoal, picked up his two young children, got back on the horse and headed for shore, each holding on for life as the icy water level increased each minute.

But it was hard to hold on with frigid fingers, so young Ruby grabbed at the horse's reins, causing it to turn about and lose its bearings. They had to get off but their father couldn't swim!

"We got off and the horse went in shore," said Ruby. "How we got on the reef I'll never know but the three of us was on that reef again," said Ruby.

Three were then stranded. Worse yet, the boy fell unconscious. "I fell off the horse," said Junior. "I got a lot of water in my lungs."

Then, someone made a wise choice.

Bill Brown was alerted. The local fisherman was known to be a very strong swimmer. One time he was showing off for his family as they stood watching from the shore. He was jumping from his boat into raging high waves, climbing back on board then diving in again.

Bill's response to the stranded White family was just as gutsy. "He swam out to get us, " said Ruby, "and he took one kid on each arm and he told my dad to hold on to his belt."

I spoke with the rescuer's daughter Edith Purdy, who still lives in the area. She described what her father saw once he had reached the stranded three.

"When Dad got there he told me that Placide was standing on the reef with each child under his arm and the tide was up to his chin," she said. "Dad said he told him, so he wouldn't panic, 'if you do what I tell you I can save you.'"

Believe it or not, through ice and freezing slush, Bill Brown made it happen. He saved all three!

"He got us out of there," said Ruby.

Amazing!

"He walked in along the reef," said Junior, "and got us out of there."

Somehow Bill had managed to wade through the frigid water on an intricate route back to shore. Quoted in print later, he said he "knew the reef like the palm of his hand."

With the water up to his chin, there were only minutes left to make the rescue. "He said 'the water's cold'," said Edith, "So he wouldn't be able to make a second trip out."

None was needed.

The unconscious Junior White was resuscitated on shore. Ruby, Junior and their father suffered from shock and exposure but all survived.

Like Junior, Ruby will never forget Bill Brown's bravery. "I think of that all the time because there were so many attempts to save us and nobody could get through! But he did."

The Mainland & Cape Breton: A Couple in Therapy

Evidence that the annexation is illegal!

It's been a rocky marriage from day one. Cape Breton and mainland Nova Scotia need counselling to mend marital rifts. Perhaps it would be best to consult a therapist who's half Cape Bretoner and half mainlander, like me? Go ahead. I'm listening.

First, let's therapeutically reflect on the relationship's history. Separatist sentiments have been present for over two centuries. The Caper

comedian General John Cabot Trail's popular parody of these sentiments ("Down with the causeway!") is rooted in the Island's record of
disadvantages. In the winter of 2000, some Islanders gathered in
Baddeck to seriously discuss becoming "an entity unto ourselves," as
Glace Bay citizen Fraser Morrison put it.

It's an attitude that echoes from way back when the two settlements
were just dating. Here's the troubled marital history: initially, the
maritime region was called Acadia. In 1713, Acadia was divided up.
Mainland Nova Scotia went under British rule, Cape Breton Island
went under French rule. It was to be called Isle Royale. The two lived
separately. After about fifty years, Cape Breton was annexed back to the
mainland. A forced marriage. It was a strained relationship. Not even
much of a honeymoon from what I hear.

In 1784, as British Loyalists arrived in Cape Breton, the mother
country decided on a separate island colony again. The interfering
mother-in-law didn't care for her precious offspring's spouse. Her wish
was respected. Separation papers were drawn up.

The island was doing all right on its own. No meagre existence in a
basement bachelor apartment for this post-divorce survivor! Heck no.
The island had a new life of its own: Lieutenant governors, administra-
tors, an executive council, and even a capital—Sydney. An official
proclamation was written out on paper granting Cape Breton its own
House of Assembly as a British Colony. Not a bad divorce settlement.
And with the influx of Scots, there were eventually enough people to
call the first Assembly into session. The first big housewarming bash to
celebrate the freedom of singlehood again. Wahoo!

But before the party could happen, it was cancelled. In 1820, the
British annexed the two colonies once again. Now, we all know the
reunited couple syndrome is a long shot. It takes a lot of work. Both
have to be very sure, right? Well, this reunion was not exactly whole-
heartedly agreed upon.

Cape Bretoners of the day were shocked at the illegal, forced remar-
riage. Dr. Bob Morgan, a respected historian with many years at the
University College of Cape Breton, has a real problem with this illegal
coupling. He told me that only a British Parliament decision could

remove a previously granted House of Assembly, which Cape Breton had. But the King and his government acted without parliament's blessing. The annexation was a shotgun wedding. "The whole thing was illegal," said Dr. Morgan, "unconstitutional."

So as for the proclamation declaring Cape Breton independent, "Is it still on the books?" I asked.

"Yeah," he said.

It seems General John actually has the law on his side in his causeway condemnation! Apparently, the island and mainland have been—technically—living in sin all these years.

Sure, Islanders fought for independence. After many failed petitions, they even hired a lawyer. "It was brought before British parliament into the Privy Council which would be like the Supreme Court now," said Dr. Morgan.

Alas, annexation would stand. The British just said "no." The British brass knew they were ignoring their own law and that Islanders had a sound case. But it all came down to the politics of Cape Breton's lucrative coal contribution, those monied mines of yesteryear. "The whole government of Nova Scotia wouldn't get responsible government without this source of income," said Dr. Morgan.

Today, the dowry disintegrated, the spouse feels used.

Nevertheless, Islanders had put the legal fight for divorce behind them. Electing people to the legislature in Halifax showed a *de facto* acceptance which may have nulled the legal separation agreement.

And yet, there was never total acquiescence. Talk of separation continued throughout the 1820s, 30s and 40s. By the 1880s, a separation resolution was passed by the Cape Breton County Council. That movement ended when its leader died of heart failure.

By 1906—more separation talk. As late as 1973, the Metropolitan Alliance for Development, the voice of most Cape Bretoners then, called for radical change including the separate province option. It was always there. A soft yearning to pack a bag and walk away, letting the screen door slam with no looking back.

MLA Paul McEwan's Cape Breton Labour Party had Island separation as one of its platforms in 1984. Dr. Morgan notes that rebellious fervour flares—understandably—when economic times are most tough on the Island.

But now, I must ask you, as someone willing to wear the title Mr. Nova Scotia Know-It-All, do you think I could sit back and watch the disintegration of our provincial paradise? No, I tell you! We cannot and must not let it happen. Surely we can work this out. I say there may have been tough times but I sense a bit of spark left in the relationship, no matter how rocky its origin. I think, deep down, there is love. Forget what happened in the past, what matters is today, right?

It's like the troubled Quebec relationship. The rest of Canada reached out to them and they chose to stay in the marital home. We can do that too, right here. Let's do more to show our fellow Nova Scotians of the northeast that their distinctiveness is understood, that we like them, and want them to stay in the fold. Not just because it's awkward divvying up the old wedding presents. But because, gosh darn it, we need each other.

We're good together. We have a history, a shared past. We have some great times to remember. That should be our key provincial goal: keeping mainlanders and Islanders together, in happy unison, sharing the wealth, in sickness and in health, with mines opened or closed, the Sydney steel plant owned or sold, and with the best of both sides of the strait merged as one. Let's make it happen. It's for a good cause(way).

The *Titanic* Captain and Us

Infamous skipper was student of Nova Scotian sailors.

Long after the massive Hollywood blockbuster, after that all-too-familiar Celine Dion pop music heartwrencher, after the tide of *Titanic* trivia rose to its fullest and ebbed to a steady flow of curiosity about anything to do with the great unsinkable ship story, THEN, and only THEN, this historical *Titanic* tie-in popped up, as if escaping the powerful wake of the media hype. It seems there is a link between that ill-fated luxury liner's captain and our very own nautical roots here in the Bluenose province.

Titanic of course went down to her watery grave on the ocean floor, in April 1912. Her Captain, Edward John Smith, spared himself the pointing fingers of the world by going down with her into the deep. It was a calamitous end to a career that began for Smith—lo and behold—under the apprenticeship of skilled Nova Scotian sailors.

The master seaman's name is headlined in a short 1912 newspaper article from the *Halifax Daily Echo*, discovered by Lynn-Marie Richard, a researcher at the Maritime Museum of the Atlantic. Dated just days after the sinking, the article's headline reads "Capt. Smith was a Windsor man!" It goes on to detail—with mistakes and facts—the *Titanic* captain's early sailing training on Nova Scotian vessels.

Just when you thought there was nothing new to learn about this sensational sinking story, along comes a new Nova Scotian footnote. To check it out, Ms. Richard's museum mate Dan Conlin put me on to a relative of the *Titanic* captain. Patricia Lacey is the author of a biographical novel called *Master of the Titanic*. Captain Smith was her great grandmother's uncle. I rang her in England. (That's Brit-talk for "I phoned her.")

Ms. Lacey told me Captain Smith was first drawn to the sea by "his half brother Joseph who was 16 years older than he was." Joseph was a master seaman. Born in 1850, Smith sailed with Joseph as a ship's boy or apprentice.

That 1912 Halifax newspaper article refers to a ship registered in Windsor called the *Princess Royal* that Smith's half brother Joseph sailed on. So the headline was wrong. The Smith on board was not actually from Windsor. He was a Smith, but he was not THE Smith. Nevertheless, Joseph was first in the *Titanic* captain's family to sail on one of our Nova Scotian vessels.

And get this: "After Capt. Smith's half-brother left this vessel," said Dan Conlin, "it hit an iceberg!"

An unfortunate family fate? Perhaps. But the *Titanic* tie tightens further. As a youth, Captain Smith himself also had stints on Nova Scotian vessels.

"He was on the *Amoy* that was registered in Halifax and he also sailed on the *Agra*, registered in Windsor," said Ms. Lacey from her home in England. "Your Windsor," she clarified.

"The vessels connected to Capt. Smith have a long succession of Nova Scotian captains," said Conlin, "where Smith was learning the ropes, literally."

There are still some dates to verify but it's likely the largely unblemished sailing career of Captain E.J. Smith was partly shaped by his early training under New Scotland skippers. And with Nova Scotian captains, it was very common that the crewmen also would be local sailors, even family members. So it seems we Bluenoses helped teach the *Titanic* skipper how to sail!

Now, don't wince at that distinction. We should be proud. He was a great sailor. Sure, a captain takes full responsibility for his ship's shape—for the cruise quality and the crew's quality. Yet, could Smith really be blamed for the *Titanic* tragedy?

Titanic's captain learned sailing from Nova Scotian seamen? Oops.

"Smith had a long and quiet and successful career up until that unfortunate night in 1912," said Dan Conlin.

"So obviously he learned a lot of things correctly, especially on smaller vessels and on sailing vessels. It's a shame there wasn't someone to teach him about large steam ships when they started to appear at the turn of the century."

No one *could* teach him. The ships were new to the world and he was already the top skipper in the Whitestar line. Someone had to be first taking the risk at the helm.

Besides, sailing vessels quadrupled in size in just ten years. The giant steamships were unfamiliar and unwieldy. Traditional sailing methods couldn't measure up to the demands of these new giants of the sea.

There were earlier warnings about manoeuvering problems. On the first voyage of *Titanic*'s sister ship *Olympic*, Captain Smith crushed the stern off a tugboat in New York Harbour. He had another accident with her in the English channel. Even when *Titanic* sailed out of Southampton she sucked two other ships off their moorings in her huge wake.

We can claim a hand in his beginning but perhaps Smith's tragic *Titanic* end was not his fault. It's a matter of some debate. The movie portrays the kinds of pressures he was under to push the untried ocean-going behemoth towards its highest speed, despite the icy obstacles the captain had to know were out there. And of course there's the matter of the ship's below-decks design, allowing incoming seawater to flow over the wall, from one open-ceiling chamber to the other. They made sinking easy.

Did our seamen teach Edward John Smith well? It seems they did. Before going to the bottom with his ship, he had risen to the top of his profession.

The Evil Dagger Woods

Murder, mystery or misnomer haunts those trees.

I still feel spinal shivers when I drive through those dark acres of thick forest. The Dagger Woods is said to be a place of evil happenings.

This eerie tract of trees closes in on an empty section of the 104 highway, between Antigonish and the village of Heatherton, on the way to Cape Breton.

It allows my car to pass through its green gauntlet but my uneasy childhood memories always surface.

"Long ago a man committed a bloody murder with a long, sharp dagger! He ran into the woods with the knife. He was never seen again!"

That's the story many locals, me included, grew up with.

The Dagger Woods story has been around a long time, in different forms. Dorothy Blythe, an amiable Halifax publisher, grew up near those dark woods, at Afton, Antigonish County. She told me she had been told by her elders that the murderer used "a pearl-handled dagger."

Her mother told her the old story of a horse that unexpectedly returned home from the Dagger Woods without its rider! Those tales still drift through Antigonish County like a floating apparition changing shapes. It's difficult to trace such a wisp of lore.

Mary L. Fraser collected those rural stories in her book *Folklore of Nova Scotia*. Fraser writes that "preternatural disturbances occurred many years ago" all through that district.

Goblins, murderers, spooks; if these woods could talk...!

Fraser claims the "usual manifestation was in the form of cries. A cry was first heard in the distance, then nearer and consequently louder, and then just at hand."

Fraser writes, "A man and his sister were driving through the Dagger Woods when they spoke one to the other of the Bochdan." The Gaelic word refers to an ancient Scottish goblin.

"Scarcely had they mentioned it," Fraser continues, "when a cry was heard a way off towards Meadow Green. To this cry they paid no attention; but a second one nearer made them more anxious; a third, within a few yards, terrified them. It was a human cry, but a hundred voices could not produce its volume."

Eewwww! No wonder I'm still spooked.

That same storyteller's father told her he was riding his horse through there in 1870 when he heard those eerie cries, sounding ever closer with each one. His horse fell down in terror, pouring sweat.

Such is the nature of century-old lore among the Highland descendants of rural Antigonish County.

There's a will to believe there that's near the strength of truth itself. Strong enough to evoke a ponderous moment in the hardest skeptics.

Or to scare the wits out of a wide-eyed young boy nervously watchful in the backseat!

But I decided to take a grown up look at that name: Dagger Woods. To confront the demons of my youth, as it were.

I summoned the rich resources of Antigonish County's wisest elders. Including my mom. She's well connected. She helped me contact the eminent historian Dr. Ray MacLean; the indomitable local history writer, since deceased, Eileen Cameron Henry; and the learned retired Judge Hugh MacPherson. He consulted long-time teacher John Archie Chisholm *and* an 1876 history of the area by Dr. J.W. MacDonald. These are some of the best keepers of oral history in them parts—a Know-It-All's dream team!

Alas, my assembled brain trust was not conclusive. The mystery remained. They offered, however, a very likely etymological explanation for the Dagger name. It may be from an English mangling of the name Dyker or Daeger.

Journalist Kingsley Brown, a neighbour of the Dagger district at Southside Harbour, expanded on that logic. He did some legwork on this name theory.

Brown knew that among the first five families that settled in the nearby Acadian village Pomquet in the early 1700s, there was a family named Daigle. The parish priest told Brown there was no record of that family in the parish register. But Mr. Brown checked with a Mr. Rogers, a very long-time resident of the Dagger district. The Heatherton elder told Brown that indeed "there *had* been a family named 'Daigle' living in that nook of the woods along the way."

Aha! So 'Daigle' was mangled into 'Dagger' over the centuries. It's possible. It seems even logical.

Consider this, however: maybe, just maybe, that early family of Daigles was the first to hear the terrorizing cries of the evil Bochdan. Or what if that ancient Celtic goblin, heard by so many over so long, was the reason the murderer—hiding in the woods with the Dagger— was never seen again?

Whatever the story, I still can't drive fast enough through the Dagger Woods.

Hickory Dickory Dock, Another Man Who Lived in Our Clock!

A Californian claim on the Halifax Town Clock.

This is a Part Two, of sorts, from a chapter in my first book, History with a Twist. *That story, about an unusual place to live, was one of the most requested at many book readings and public talks I gave. It was the first story of the 'Nova Scotia Know-It-All' style that I had told on CBC Radio's "Information Morning." It was even before the preposterous title was handed me! Yet, the twists continue. Here I am, five or six years later, stumbling across another new slant to that nostalgic trip through time.*

W ho would have imagined when I toured Halifax's historic Town Clock on Citadel Hill some years ago with a man who once lived inside it, that I'd later discover another Halifax clock-dweller from two centuries ago? A woman in Santa Rosa, California, just north of San Francisco, contacted me to say she is directly de-scended from the first resident of our tick-tock tourist attraction, built in 1803. Truly!

Donna Dightman Rudin's family website, based in California, features a big background photo of Nova Scotia's famous Town Clock, complete with an audio file of its chimes. Our hillside timepiece is an important Dightman family symbol. Just as it has special meaning for Dennis Gill who lived there in the late 1950s.

He had been my tour guide inside the large clock-keeper's quarters in the base of the clock tower. He was visiting the home where he lived as a boy. His father was the Citadel's clock caretaker back then. For Dennis, revisiting the clock was nostalgic. Together, we climbed the steep stairs of the bell tower, past the clock works, the pendulum closet, and up to the open belfry.

He recalled that changing the time on the old clock had been a family affair. "There'd be times when the whole family would come up," said Dennis, "and my father and one of the men from the Citadel would coordinate their activity because somebody actually had to go outside on a catwalk and physically adjust the hands of the clock."

It was a magical tour back in time.

Donna Dightman Rudin's tour through time stretched back much further. In 1998, her family research brought her from California to that same city timepiece on the hill.

Our Town Clock was the home of her great, great, great, great, great, grandfather James Dechman, the first of her family in North America.

She had traced the Dightman name from early Californian pioneers up to Calais, Maine. A call to the Colchester Historical Museum in Truro helped her dig one layer deeper, back to Nova Scotia where the Dightman name was traditionally spelled 'Dechman' though her ancestors here had pronounced it "Dightman" (Dite-man).

In Thomas B. Akins' book *History of Halifax City* (1895), Donna learned that her pioneering relative James Dechman was a skilled carpenter and lived in (and she thinks he even helped to build) our Town Clock. She was thrilled to see his name on the outside plaque just below the clock building.

Her trip here was joyous. She had travelled across the continent and back in time, two centuries. By phone from her home in California, she described a feeling of coming full-circle, of feeling complete, of coming home.

"Oh pretty overwhelming! It still is today. Just coming home to Halifax, just to be there was overwhelming," she said. "It's like I knew I had to go to experience Nova Scotia."

"Why?" I asked.

"I don't know that answer but I have been driven my entire life to find that answer, and then to be there…"

Her voice wavered with emotion. "I had to come home," she wept. "It's like a starting place."

Although it was her first time in the province, she spoke tenderly of Nova Scotia as if she belonged here. For her, Halifax is her family home, her ancestral home.

"It's like a healing or a completeness that you feel when you've got your family history," she said.

While here, she visited the original Dightman—or rather, Dechman—land grant in Upper Musquodoboit, Halifax County. Without any prior warning, she drove into the driveway of John and Emma Dightman—brother and sister—still living on the same pioneer ground. They were amazed and glad to meet this long-lost relative and invited her to stay the night.

Halifax's Town Clock: two bedrooms, heat, lights, time included.

Another distant relative in Halifax took Donna to Sunday services at St Matthew's Church, where the original clock-keeper had been a Deacon. She wanted to see what the congregation calls the Kirk Fiddle. The old wooden cello kept behind the altar was handcrafted by James Dechman Jr. and first used in church services in 1817. A Symphony Nova Scotia cellist played the old Kirk Fiddle during its rededication in 1998. For Donna, seeing the cello in its glass case "was quite exciting."

"It's a beautiful instrument, lovingly taken care of," she said. "The congregation cherishes it, it's part of their history, it's still playable, it's had several restorations."

Her connection to these master craftsmen, church leaders, and clock-keepers of old—the Dechman family—leaves her feeling "extreme pride."

"These are the pioneers, the founders of Halifax," she said. "These individuals helped make Halifax what it is today, they were part of the culture, part of the church. James Dechman the pioneer was a member of the North British Society which had many charity functions. They were a civic minded family," she said.

For her, our clock tolls for the Dightman family. Her visit to it was a personal pilgrimage. "I got to hear it chime," she said. "It tugs at your heart strings. It echoes a song that's been played for many, many years."

It was a wistful sentiment from a voice at the end of a phone line on the far side of the continent.

"I left my heart in Halifax," she said.

Master of Illumination

A friend of Edison brings good things to light.

This true tale about a pioneer of electric lighting comes in two parts, bright and brighter. After telling part one on the radio, new information was shone upon me. Hence, part deux. Amazingly, the extra info came from a continent away and it casts more revealing light on this interesting illuminator. Enjoy! And don't read in the dark, you'll hurt your eyes.

Whose bright idea was that, to illuminate the towers and cables of Halifax's Macdonald Bridge at night? Or the upper reaches of the Empire State Building for that matter? Exterior spotlights are a universal architectural standard invented by a clever illuminating engineer—the first to hold that title—from Kentville. He was very bright.

Walter D'Arcy Ryan, born April 17, 1870, was a pioneer lighting designer, the first to light up Niagara Falls, world fairs, and American city streets.

Surprised? So was I. But this checks out. I'm not in the dark about this brilliant guy. Oh yeah, we can claim him!

I sought out and spoke with a modern-day lighting designer with a major American architectural firm called CUH2A, in Princeton, New Jersey. Jill Mulholland loves light. She also enjoyed researching this pioneer of her craft, Walter D. Ryan.

"I think I would have loved to have met him," she told me. "Most of the methods he pioneered in the way light is applied to architecture are the foundation concepts of lighting today," she said.

In 1907, Ryan used carbon arc searchlights with colour filters to illuminate Niagara Falls. In 1909, he installed searchlights on the stately Singer Building, then the tallest building in New York City.

"He was the first to indirectly light buildings," said Mulholland. "Before that, buildings had incandescent lightbulbs screwed into the walls, and the windows and domes were outlined like little dots."

Our Walter Ryan was cleverly creative.

"He took lights and hid them in the buildings' architecture and he bounced the light off the foundations. We see this all the time today and we never think twice about it but at the time it was a very new, radical effect," said the lighting specialist.

As a young engineer in 1892, Ryan went to Lynn, Massachusetts to join the Thomson-Houston company which later fused into General Electric. In 1899, he organized an illuminating engineering lab for G.E.

One of his most fantastic lighting displays was for the Panama Pacific International Exposition, the world's fair, at San Francisco in 1915. Inspired by the colours of the Northern Lights which he could have seen in his youth in Nova Scotia, he tried to duplicate their effect.

His rainbow scintillator device shot powerful, colourful searchlights skyward at night, against a high wall of shimmering steam.

It had forty-eight 36-inch navy boat search lights, each with colour filters. The lights beamed up into "the steam from a locomotive and imitated the Aurora Borealis."

Ryan had rigged a locomotive to run with its wheels lifted so it remained in place while producing steam.

"He was the first to use indirect lighting on the surface. He picked and collected different effects, perfected them scientifically, and made them work," said Mulholland.

That 1915 fair also featured the brilliant Tower of Jewels, a tall structure in ornate Italian Renaissance style. People passed under its archway to enter the fair.

Built with "450 million board feet of lumber and a phenomenal amount of steel, it was huge."

But Walter Ryan made it a wondrous, sparkling sensation. "He got the architects to hang these leaded crystals from Austria off the tower, said Mulholland. "He hid searchlights on top of the other buildings and shone them onto the jewels. They were different colours and backed with mirrored reflectors and they flashed and shimmered in the night time."

Walter D'Arcy Ryan of Kentville: Thomas Edison's illuminating pal.

Imagine the oohs and ahhhs of wonder!

Ryan was a rare scientific-artistic mix. The General Electric Archives has him educated at Kentville Academy, then at Professor Currey's school and St. Mary's College, both in Halifax. He went on to Memramcook College, N.B., then military school in Quebec.

Halifax's genial genealogical genius Terry Punch tells me Walter D'Arcy Ryan's parents, James and Mary, and his grandparents, John and Catherine, and two of his siblings are buried at the Catholic cemetery in Kentville. His father was a dry goods merchant in that town.

This illuminating scientist from the Annapolis Valley was a personable sort. Obituary descriptions cast a good light on his character.

"They describe him as a friendly fraternal fellow," said Mulholland. "To be able to pull off the things he did, the budgets he got, he had to be fairly well-liked and talented."

He lectured and published widely. In 1933, he designed the lighting spectacles of the Century of Progress world exhibition at Chicago.

A year later, he was gone. He died March 14, 1934. A General Electric obituary said he was the first to make artificial illumination both a science and an art.

Walter D'Arcy Ryan was buried on Saint Patrick's Day in Parkwood Cemetery in Schenectady, New York. He was one of Nova Scotia's bright lights in the big city.

〜

An interesting story huh? I was happy with it. Sure, it's always nicer to get the goods from a family member but I determined there were no Ryan descendants in Kentville. If there were any still living, they could be anywhere in the world. I even checked listings for Schenectady, New York where he had lived and worked. No relevant Ryan relatives to be found. So that was it. Shut off the lights and go home. But then, some sparks. Apparently, someone who heard me tell the above story happened to notice a genealogical inquiry posted somewhere in the internet's cyber world and responded to it. The inquiry originated from the American west coast.

The 1915 San Francisco World's Fair, lighted by a Nova Scotian inventor.

I guess my name was mentioned over the fibre optic back fence, and the next thing I know I'm getting electronic mail from a far-off member of Ryan's family asking what I knew about him that they didn't. I was pleasantly shocked. It was like small-town gossip writ large. My story had gone out into the ether but was repeated until it met a concerned party and came back to me with fascinating new detail. Really neat stuff that even the lighting specialist Jill Mulholland didn't know when publishing her professional journal article on Walter D. Ryan.

This family connection shed a whole new light on this illuminating Nova Scotian, as I learned when I called the Ryan family in Livermore, California.

I reached Virginia (Ryan) Durrant, Walter D'Arcy Ryan's daughter! A sharp 87, she gladly grabbed her portable phone, searched out her father's old book of photos and sat down to describe for me that 1915 rainbow scintillator device.

"It has the rainbow-like things coming out of the sky around it and the Tower of Jewels in the middle of it; it's beautiful," she said in a clear, intelligent voice.

"It has all the different colours radiating out from the base; sixteen different colours of light," she said. "It's just gorgeous!"

The Tower of Jewels was Ryan's idea too: A tall, ornate building at the San Francisco fair with hundreds of Austrian crystals and reflectors hanging from it, sparkling in coloured searchlights.

But some skeptics thought the effect wouldn't work. Ryan had his doubting Thomas: Thomas Edison himself!

"He and Edison were good friends," said Virginia, casually. "My dad invited him to come to the Exposition as his guest because Edison didn't believe he (Ryan) could do what he said he was going to do!"

Virginia laughed at the memory, as old as it was.

Turns out, the doubting Thomas Edison was pleasantly shocked when he saw Ryan's electrical artistry. "After that he was a strong supporter of my dad," said Virginia. "I guess there were a lot of doubters. No one had seen it done before; it was something new."

How many Nova Scotians does it take to impress a lightbulb inventor? Apparently just one. And his wife.

"Mother and Dad had been at the Edisons' home and I had a picture of my father and Edison taken out in front of Dad's lab at Schenectady," said Virginia. "I had a doll that was given me by Edison; my sister got doll furniture."

Ryan was among the luminaries of illumination. Edison had his lightbulb, Ryan had his headlight. Early automobile drivers were thankful for the invention.

"He came out with a seal-beamed headlight, a non-glare, that went way down the road," said Virginia, "and we got all kinds of letters from people everywhere; how wonderful it was for them to be able to see at night."

As a little girl, Virginia rode with her dad as he test-drove the new headlight. He fended off offers from General Motors. His patent lasted 17 years.

Ryan also lit up Washington's famous Lincoln Memorial monument.

"I remember mother telling about how he brought a model of it home and then they would work with it to get the lights right, so it wouldn't shadow," said Virginia.

Wonderful! A local boy makes good south of the border. But this light man's story doesn't go dark there. It's about to reflect back to its source. Remember, in part one of this light man's tale, I told of Walter Ryan's family gravesite in Kentville's Catholic cemetery. His grandparents and siblings who died young are buried there alongside his parents. I've since learned that Ryan's mother had passed away on a train bound for San Francisco. She was on her way to see her son's magnificent lighting spectacles at that 1915 Exposition. She never made it to California.

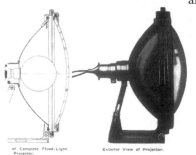

The electric non-glare headlight: a Nova Scotian invention?

But now, 86 years later, her son's family in California is planning a cross-continent trek here to pay a visit at the family gravesite. Virginia Ryan and her daughter Carolyn— Walter Ryan's granddaughter—were thrilled to learn of the graves. They wanted to see them. By the time you are reading this, they will have travelled to Nova Scotia to touch the family headstones, to read the inscriptions, and to walk through the old town where Walter D'Arcy Ryan, the first illuminating engineer, was born.

That Lucky Sip of Whiskey

How a belt of booze saved a soldier's life in Italy.

L et me guess. You think of Remembrance Day and you're thinking of old men in ill-fitting uniforms on a cold, damp day. You think of wet leaves, poppy pin-pricks, chilling wind gusts and snapping flags. But how many of us are really able to understand what that man in that war did? For us. Our discomfort at cold, outdoor memorial ceremonies once a year pales in comparison to the survival stories our veterans can tell. We owe them much more than that yearly token trip to the cenotaph.

Even though he survived the so-called 'forgotten war,' the Allies' invasion of Italy, 82-year-old Meredith Shankel of Halifax still has the physical wounds to assure that *he* never forgets. It was a World War Two campaign, overshadowed by the big push into France—the beaches of Normandy and all that. Italy was Hell for a lot of our men.

In 1944, Meredith was no longer just a junior bank employee. He was an officer with the *Princess Louise Fuseliers*, in the 5th Canadian Infantry, in a convoy of ships, sailing into trouble.

A German torpedo hit and sank one of the ships. Shankel remembers soldiers being dragged from the drink onto other ships in the convoy. Due to all the extra mouths to feed, every soldier on board lost one meal per day for the rest of the voyage. Ironically, once they arrived in Naples, Italy and marched to Altamura, they faced a comparative feast!

They were camped and training for battle at the front—the calm before the storm. It was his first Christmas overseas and the meal was festive. "Turkey and all the trimmings," said Shankel, "half a bottle of Canadian beer per officer. It was great!"

The wartime Christmas dinner included menu items named for the officers. "I remember mine," he said. "It was Shankel's plum pudding."

The food and fun were a nice break.

The men were soft and weary after their long voyage and the arduous

Meredith Shankel: a simple sip saved his life.

march to Altamura, staggering under heavy rifles and machine guns. But the dinner ended. It was time to push into Italy's interior to do battle.

At the infamous Monte Cassino—an old monastery on a hill held by the Germans—enemy mortar fire rained down heavily. The calm was definitely over. This was the storm. Pinned down, Shankel and his comrades couldn't move around it by day.

"You'd hear these convoys of trucks and tanks and everything grinding in the night."

Enemy fire blasted all around. Getting killed was easy to do. Their lives depended often on just luck. Meredith Shankel remembers, vividly, one very narrow escape from death that was so close it seemed absurd.

Gunfire erupted everywhere. Exploding shells sent geysers of soil skyward. Shankel started across the battle field to a shell hole where a soldier was cooking up field rations for anyone with time to chow down.

The close call that came next still shakes him. On his way to the food, he heard the voice of a comrade in a slit trench. "'Hey Canada,' he yelled, 'how'd you like a drink of whiskey?'" Shankel chose a drink over food and joined the man in his trench.

"We were having a drink and the shells came over, landed in the shell hole where the fellow was cooking the meal, blew him all to the devil and…"

His voice quivered with emotion, his eyes watered. "A drink of whiskey saved my life," he said, still bewildered.

But, later, he wasn't so lucky.

The troops pushed past Monte Cassino, up the Liri Valley. Under heavy fire, they breached German defenses and poured through.

At Luigi, Italy, Shankel was coming out of an officers' meeting about regrouping, holding a map and papers. He and his driver faced a shower of shells and ducked under a vehicle.

"I was bending over and the blood was falling down on the papers," said Shankel in a shaky voice.

He recalled his driver's reaction. "'I think I've been hit,' he said to me." The veteran struggled with emotion as he spoke.

"I said, 'I know bloody well I've been hit,'" he said, in trembling voice.

Thirteen pieces of shrapnel had sliced into his body. "Some in my wrists, some in my hands; a piece went through my leg, three pieces in my eye and a piece through my lip," he said, regaining himself.

One tooth was smashed out and paining badly. But in the base hospital in Italy, the nurse informed him it was no time to seek dental help. "She said, 'you can't get a dentist. It's Christmas,'" said Shankel. A whole year of battle had passed.

The wounded officer demanded an abstraction. "So, they did take it out—on Christmas morning!"

He had come full circle, Christmas to Christmas, seeing a lot of death and destruction in between.

Once patched up and out of combat, he continued in the service till war's end on ship's conducting duty: sailing our troops home, then returning German prisoners back overseas. He also sailed on several ships bringing the war brides home. In all, Meredith Shankel crossed the Atlantic a total of 52 times—26 round trips!

Once home, he married, returned to work and eventually retired as a senior bank official at a main branch in Halifax.

Like many Canadian soldiers, he did his part for our way of life. Let's remember them—beyond Remembrance Day.

Our Front Page Challenger

Nova Scotian newshound was
top contributor to TV show.

(Applause!)
"All right, we'll meet our next challenger after you hear
about the story in headline form."
– Fred Davis, Moderator of F.P.C.

R emember Front Page Challenge on CBC TV? Even as kids we watched those two bow-tied intellectual newsmen Gordon Sinclair and Pierre Berton, and their elegant, intelligent female co-panelist Betty Kennedy as they guessed at the mystery newsmakers of the night. Of course, we didn't have cable so we had no choice in our viewing. And good thing. We actually learned things from Front Page. Imagine! Learning from TV!

It was the world's longest running panel show—38 years—kept alive by interesting, newsy, contributed story suggestions. And the champion contributor of hundreds, perhaps thousands, of story ideas over three decades was "Agnes Miller of Kentville, Nova Scotia."

That was a phrase the panelists heard often. Some nights, both stories on the show came from "Agnes Miller of Kentville, Nova Scotia." When I visited her at her home, she told me that close to a hundred of her suggestions were used on that TV panel program: A priest protesting the American draft, the victory of Robert Mugabe in Rhodesia, the Nova Scotian M.P. Elmer MacKay's claim that Tory offices had been bugged…and many, many more.

Agnes read me her handwritten entries in her story scribbler. "'Offshore oil deal signed by Nova Scotia'; That's when John Buchanan was premier," she said. "'Iron ore mines closed in Schefferville, Quebec'; That's when I was a double winner."

Agnes was a stay-at-home wife and mother most of her life. The depression and the war and the 'times' meant she didn't have a career. She spent a few years, way back, as a proofreader at Kentville Publishing. If starting again today, she assured me, she'd have been a gritty, globetrotting reporter. I believe her.

She loves to read nonfiction—all the national and local newspapers and books on World War Two.

Cantankerous old Gordon Sinclair in his bad comb-over hairdo and loud checkered jacket loved asking the mystery guests, "How much do you make?"

For Agnes, the answer would be 25 bucks per story used on air, later raised to $50. It was a cottage industry. For close to a hundred stories used, she must have earned a few thousand dollars over thirty years of contributing.

"Once they accepted one of mine, that was it; I didn't ever look back! But," she laughed, "I never, never—at that time—ever in the world, thought I'd be on the show or meet them!"

A newspaper clipper's dream come true! Agnes Miller of Kentville, Nova Scotia was invited to appear as a mystery guest on the program she had been writing to half her life. In 1985, Front Page Challenge came to Nova Scotia to do a broadcast from Halifax. They sent a car to Kentville to pick up Agnes.

The smooth-voiced moderator, the late Fred Davis, intoned the usual introduction. The panel was ready. Then a booming announcer's voice (Frank Cameron) secretly informed viewers at home of the next mystery guest: "Where would we have been," the big voice asked, "without our next challenger?—Agnes Miller of Kentville, Nova Scotia."

Ironically, the panel was stumped. They didn't guess that the story was about the woman who had sent them so many stories.

During the interview segment that followed the guessing, Betty Kennedy asked Agnes if her clipping craze came from a journalism background. "No, I went to a little one-room country school," she said, "to grade eleven. But we had some wonderful teachers."

After I talked with Agnes about her TV appearance sixteen years ago, I couldn't resist calling up Betty Kennedy, a newly-minted senator in

Ottawa. In the heady first days of her new appointment, I wanted to see if the distinguished senator still remembered this humble champion contributor from her Front Page Challenge years.

When I said, "Agnes Miller of Kentville, Nova Scotia," recognition was instant.

"She was remarkable," said the senator, "and her stories were always very good ones. Many of her suggestions did get used."

"After a while they would say, 'And that story comes from Agnes Miller' and I'm sure we almost wondered if she was part of our staff!" The senator chuckled at the memory.

Agnes Miller (centre front) with Front Page panel and guests.

Front Page Challenge folded in 1995. Agnes now sends her clippings to me—packages of them at a time. Each week, on CBC Radio's Information Morning, I invite Nova Scotians around the province to contribute story ideas. I've been very lucky. Response is great every week: e-mails, phone calls, faxes, and the occasional letters. Agnes is probably once again the champion contributor. Her suggestions come in the form of bundles of clippings in big over-stuffed envelopes. Mailed in the old fashioned way. With stamps.

In fact, you can see one of her letters to me, incorporated into the front cover design of the first Nova Scotia Know-It-All book, *History with a Twist*. So Agnes Miller of Kentville, Nova Scotia is once again on the Front Page, so to speak.

Thanks for your help Agnes.

Mission to Africa

*An Annapolis Valley woman
sacrifices all to help* Amistad *slaves.*

Into the teeming jungles of Africa a white woman bravely walked, 160 years ago. One of the first missionaries to go there, Eliza Ruggles of Dempsey Corner, Kings County had entangled herself in American history's tragic *Amistad* affair.

If you missed Stephen Spielburg's movie version of the true tale, *Amistad* was a Spanish vessel illegally carrying African captives in 1839. Spain, Britain, and America had signed treaties banning the slave trade years earlier. The smuggled captives were actually African freemen, from Sierra Leone.

They broke their chains, overcame and killed their captors, and seized control of the ship. But, unused to sailing, the Amistad captives were easily overtaken and arrested by a U.S. Navy vessel. They were jailed in New Haven, Connecticut, and accused of murder and piracy!

A two-year legal wrangle ensued as the Africans lived in deplorable conditions behind bars. They knew no one. They spoke only Mende, the language of their homeland. Their plight seemed hopeless. Some became sick and died.

Finally, passionate arguments to the Supreme Court by former president John Quincy Adams (played by Anthony Hopkins in the movie) won the day for the suffering Mende people. Found to be illegal prisoners, they were finally freed.

That's where our Nova Scotian Eliza Ruggles came in. She courageously sailed with the freed *Amistad* slaves on board the vessel *Gentleman* to live with them in the jungle. She felt it was her calling.

Eliza was born in 1817 to William and Mary Ruggles. The birth left her mother dead, so Eliza's grandmother cared for her until she was twelve. Then they both made the long, rough journey to Brantford,

Ontario where William and his new wife had moved.

At a Methodist camp meeting there, Eliza converted to the faith. She married Rev. William Raymond, a travelling American evangelist, and embraced the cause of the Anti-Slavery Association. Poverty-stricken, they survived an arduous journey south, all the way to Connecticut.

Eliza Ruggles Raymond Banks: first female missionary to Africa.

As a Congregationalist minister, Eliza (Ruggles) Raymond wanted to help the Mende resettle. She and her husband were committed to their cause. But her life in the wet, rugged jungle conditions proved emotionally and physically draining.

Her descriptions of her daily struggles are poured out in her old letters kept at the *Amistad* Research Centre at Dillard University in New Orleans. Dr. Cliff Johnson, who helped create that centre was also an advisor to *Amistad*, the movie.

From his home in New Orleans, he told me how Eliza and her husband were part of a small group who accompanied the Mende back to their homeland. She wrote those letters as reports to the American Missionary Association. Dr. Johnson said that the missionaries fought against jungle conditions and against each other. The group splintered. Their leader, Rev. James Steel, and two Black missionaries walked out.

"For a long time," said Dr. Johnson, "it was just Raymond and his wife (Eliza) with eight or ten of the former *Amistad* captives. They were pretty much alone, and they were starting to build a Church, a mission, and start a school."

Heavy rains and the extreme heat of jungle life diminished Eliza's health. She had a child there that didn't survive. She became ill, and returned a couple of times to her in-laws' home in America to recover her health. Her husband, Rev. Raymond, remained in the jungle receiving letters that Eliza wrote him from her sickbed. Later, she lost another child, and her suffering deepened. Dr. Johnson told me that just as Eliza was again recovering in America, more tragedy struck.

"She wasn't well. She had a nervous breakdown. She was concerned whether or not she'd go back because of the state of her health," he said.

Eliza's decision not to return to the jungle was made when her husband died of yellow fever in 1848. She came home to Nova Scotia, a 31-year-old childless widow, to stay with her sister in Dempsey Corner.

Now home, her broken spirit began to mend.

She met a man named Phineas Banks from nearby Aylesford. In time, Eliza became Mrs. Banks. Then came more children, replacing the ones she had lost. Her health improved, her family grew, her life moved on. Nova Scotia—her homeland—had renewed her.

But when she had grandchildren, Eliza paid homage to her past by teaching them to count in the Mende tongue she had learned in her earlier life. And a physical reminder of that time still remains.

A brilliantly-coloured window, dedicated by her family to her first husband's missionary service, still shines down upon the altar at the Aylesford Baptist Church.

Eliza died at 91. Her gravestone, just beyond the church, reads "Missionary to Africa, 1842."

Johnny Miles' Marathon Memories

A Cape Breton runner still recalls the greatest race of his life.

The oldest living winner of the famous Boston Marathon—Nova Scotia's celebrated Johnny Miles—still remembered details of his incredible victory 75 years afterward. When I reached him by phone at his senior's home in Hamilton, Ontario, the former runner had just turned 95—quite a Johnny milestone, if you will. During that call in the fall of 2000, the marathon champ shared with me some faded memories of that celebrated race in 1926. He remembered the footwear that carried him to his victory.

"A pair of sneakers," he said in his wavering, old man's voice on the long distance line. "They were very light."

How much did they cost?

"98 cents," he said. "I bought them in the Co-operators store in North Sydney."

Imagine that! I chuckled at the price. Then I asked him that cliché sports reporter question, "How did it feel to win?"

"It felt very good," he said simply.

I'll bet it did. Because Johnny Miles certainly paid his dues. Born in 1905 in Halifax, England and taken to Cape Breton as an infant, his family settled in Sydney Mines where his father was a coal miner until he went overseas in World War One. Eleven-year-old Johnny had to go down in the mines to work to feed the family. For three years he went to school and then worked the 4:00 P.M. to midnight shift underground, six days a week.

There's endurance training for any athlete.

Floyd Williston, author of *Johnny Miles—Nova Scotia's Marathon King*, told me Miles started running as a boy. By phone, from his home in Manitoba, the author explained how young Miles trained while driving the horse-drawn delivery wagon for the local grocery store.

"His father made the reins extra long," said Floyd. "He would get out of the wagon with the long reins and run behind the horse," he said. "He was often seen like that on the streets of Sydney Mines."

Running with horse power!

Young Miles had never run a 26-mile marathon until that April in 1926 when he showed up at the starting line in Bean Town. The twenty year old was going up against his running hero—Albin Stenroos of Finland, the Olympic marathon champion. Miles had worshipped this runner, keeping a 1924 picture of his hero in his pocket for two years.

"It was his ambition to meet Stenroos, not to beat Stenroos," said Floyd.

The race began. The crowd of runners surged through the Boston streets. Johnny Miles followed his father's advice to hang back, behind the lead runner Stenroos, and stay alongside the number two runner in the pack, a runner named Demar. But when he saw that Demar was not about to make a move forward, Miles decided to act alone, despite the stern advice of his father ringing in his ears.

Miles increased his pace, pulling up alongside the lead runner, Stenroos.

"He ran with him for a minute or so," said Floyd, "and then Johnny noticed that Stenroos was tiring and that he may be getting the notorious stitch in his side."

Intending to gain on his competitor's pain, Miles made his final, crucial move at the traditional do-or-die turning point in the Boston Marathon.

"At Heartbreak Hill he passed Stenroos," said Floyd, "and never looked back for fear Stenroos might be on his heels!"

With mother and father cheering him on, Johnny Miles beat the Olympic champion to the finish line by four minutes!

This Nova Scotian runner had set a Boston Marathon record. His victory was big news, splashed across newspapers everywhere, including Stenroos' hometown in Finland. What a win! Even Stenroos called him a great runner.

However…disaster was to follow. One year later, Miles set out to repeat his swift-footed victory but dropped from the race, enduring scorn from the press.

According to Floyd Williston, the biographer, Miles' father had shaved down the rubber soles of his running shoes to make them lighter. That also made them very thin where the rubber met the road. And that year, Boston's streets had new asphalt which badly burned Miles' feet. He left the race early and reporters called him a quitter; a 'one-win wonder.'

Determined to restore his reputation, Miles ran the marathon again in 1929. Like in the first race, he pulled ahead of the pack at just the right time, and snatched another sweet victory with more than a two minute margin! He was a double winner! He proved he was the real thing—that the first win was no fluke. One reporter actually apologized

Johnny Miles ran many miles, beating the best in Boston, twice!

to Miles in person and in print.

His running career continued until 1935, including two Olympic games for Canada. He did well but missed the medals. Most of his working life he held a high position with a farm machine manufacturing company in Ontario. He was inducted into the Order of Canada in 1983 and was a special guest at the 100th running of the Boston Marathon in 1996.

When I phoned him out of the blue, the old marathon marvel was willing to entertain questions again from one more inquisitive media type, more than seven decades after his thrilling first place finish.

In life, as in running, I guess Johnny Miles learned to pace himself well.

Armdale's Renaissance Man

Revisiting Halifax's grand era of shovel production. Dig it?

The renaissance man. Such an image, that title portrays! Master of many things, knower of much knowledge. No, it's not me. I'm just Mr. Know-It-All—no relation to 'renaissance man.' We had such a bloke in the province once, though. Born in 1843 and educated privately in Halifax and Boston, E. Lawson Fenerty was a captain of early Nova Scotia industry and—among many other things—an internationally recognized, award-winning inventor. This fascinating fellow once ran factories on the pleasant hills of Armdale, overlooking Halifax Harbour's North West Arm.

His is a grand story. And I have a family 'in.'

His granddaughter is still on the old family land. Phyllis Fenerty's house sits on Fenerty Road, near a babbling stream that still criss-crosses under streets off St. Margaret's Bay Road, flowing

Nova Scotia's E. L. Fenerty had a handle on the shovel market.

down to Chocolate Lake, where an old Fenerty factory once stood, at the end of Crescent Street.

Phyllis, eighty-something, spry, and proud of her past, described Lawson Fenerty's most lucrative invention by reading from a worn and torn page amply covered in inky quill script—her grandfather's handwriting.

"I invented a new shovel, patenting it in the principle countries of the world, and selling an interest in these patents to several gentlemen," he wrote.

Selling the shares raised the money to "design and build a special machine for making the new shovels."

Simple, yet ingenious.

In 1886 those Nova Scotian-made shovels were sold all over Britain and Europe. Check your garage! You may have a dusty old Fenerty shovel, perhaps marked 'Halifax Shovel Company.'

Imagine that spacious, barn-like, wooden factory of the latter 1800s. Phyllis Fenerty remembers it in its final days, when she was a little girl. "It was large, with stacks and stacks of shovels and a great deal of machinery whirring around, and belts and things," she said.

The shovel business was apparently booming—or deepening. Wagons carted off loads of them; bundles of wooden handles and metal blades. Lawson Fenerty made money—in spades. He also made money in axes, carriage axles, and shingle nails.

He unearthed many inventorly ways to make a buck. Like the "Peerless Club" self-fastening skate that strapped on your boot (1869). His new brush-making machine had patents in countries all over the world, including Belgium. His skates and shovels won gold, silver, and bronze medals from international and domestic exhibitions.

He was much more practical than that other Fenerty inventor Charles, a first cousin once re-moved who preceded E. Lawson. Charles Fenerty— a resident of Sackville—came up with the world's first bit of pulp paper, made from wood fibre. His creative genius is also documented. But he was a dreamer with little capital for mass production. Rather than patent his new paper from wood pulp, he gave away his idea in the newspaper. Let's just say he didn't need his cousin's shovel to fill his bank account after that. Lawson Fenerty was as creative but more practical than the pulp paper inventor.

Original patent sketch of Fenerty shovel design.

They called Lawson "King Edward" because he had an Edward VII look about him. "He was a big jolly man, very extroverted, very smart, full of jokes," said Phyllis.

Now here's the renaissance part I mentioned: *Who's Who and Why*, 1914, lists Lawson Fenerty as a monthly magazine columnist, a writer of poetry, composer of the song "Our Canada" (which Phyllis used to play on piano), an amateur boxer, model yacht builder and racer, and Halifax County councillor in the early 1890s.

As a sports writer, he wrote about cricket and English rugby. As a corporal with the Garrison Artillery, he once did guard duty at Gun Wharf in Halifax during the Fenian Raids.

"Well rounded" we would call him, today.

"He had an inventive mind," said Phyllis, "he didn't dream; he put things into action."

That, he did.

His shovel factory closed in 1927. He died several years later.

But a newly-minted plaque pays homage to Fenerty's renaissance period. It's installed at the new park, at the top of Fenerty Road, near the origin of the gushing brook that once powered the factory that gave life to an early Nova Scotian industry: Fenerty shovels. A true renaissance man, Lawson Fenerty dug deep into life.

When the World Comes to Town

A passionate priest creates a global village in Antigonish.

L et's talk cultural contrast times ten. Picture a gathering featuring reddish Celtic complexions and traditional tartan kilts in Nova Scotia's Highland Heart—Antigonish. Now mingle in the dark-hued faces and vibrantly coloured robes of visiting students from Africa and India. The mixture of accents and customs can bring a smile. It's an annual, marvelous, incongruous cultural treat to behold, brought to us by the daring mind of the great Dr. Moses M. Coady.

Coady was born into rural poverty in 1882 along the banks of Cape Breton's Margaree River. He became a Catholic priest and professor at his alma mater, St. Francis Xavier University in Antigonish. That's where his famous social outreach program, the Antigonish Movement, attracted students from around the globe.

The Coady International Institute on that campus has been welcoming foreign students for over forty years. Its innovative programs sprang from Coady's famous Antigonish Movement of the 1930s, 40s and 50s.

Moses Coady was a big man of great energy, the driving force behind his self-help movement. His innovation caught the attention of the world.

Standing on the pioneering work of the fiery Father Jimmy Tompkins in the 1920s, Coady had an obvious physical and philosophical strength about him. Highly learned, he was educated in Rome and in Washington. But his heart was with the little guy. He worked his whole life to bring economic power to the common folk of the Maritimes through credit unions, fishermen's unions, and co-op stores.

This brilliant priest, professor, and orator wanted folks to know they could be what the title of his book, *Masters of Their Own Destiny*, said they could be. A lofty goal for some of us today who begrudgingly leave the couch to change the channel! But the Coady era was special. His staff at the university's celebrated Extension Department—many of them women—were inspired by his vision.

Dr. Moses M. Coady: a 'white collar' worker for blue collar folk.

Along with Coady, they launched study clubs, opened a mail-order library and published pamphlets for the impoverished fishermen, lumbermen, miners, and farmers of northeastern Nova Scotia. It was anti-ivy league. It was a 'people's school.' The university even launched Antigonish's CJFX Radio to broadcast adult education programs. Rural groups listened in, gathered around kitchen radios in distant farmhouses.

The movement taught workers to challenge market forces, to work together to wrest a greater profit from their products and labours. It was radical thought for a Catholic priest back then—or even today, I'd wager. Many clergy helped Coady, but some opposed him. Other critics called him Communist. Commercial interests tried to stamp out his 'share the wealth' ideas. Yet he travelled North America spreading the co-operative gospel with his unique zeal. In one 1950 address, Coady's voice was firm and articulate as he spoke into the microphone.

"I mean an organization of economic society," he said, "where every man and woman will have their fair share of the wealth we all help to create." He sounded clear and committed. "The possibilities of economic co-operation are unlimited!"

Then his voice boomed. "That is the activity that will change the world!"

Coady's dramatic oratory rallied the masses but also touched the individual.

Sister Irene Doyle worked with the larger-than-life priest. Her respect and pride in knowing him are still evident these many years later. I visited her in Antigonish at Bethany, the large, looming brick building on the hill behind the hospital where the Sisters of St. Martha—many elderly and retired—reside. Sister Doyle, white-haired, soft-spoken, eighty-something, described for me Coady's powerful, parabolic way with words.

He often used story to make his point—like the one about the ship stranded in a salty sea, signalling another vessel, asking where to get fresh water. "And they got the message back, 'Let down your buckets where you are,'" said Sister Doyle.

As the story goes, the crew was doubtful but someone decided to try it. Sure enough, the ship was at the mouth of a great freshwater river and the crew's thirst was quenched when they let down their buckets where they were. It was classic Coadyism. Simple but powerful. It was a favourite lesson of his. Make what you have work for you.

This philosophy was the movement's inspiration. It inspired foreign students from as far as Asia to travel, unsolicited, to the small campus in the small town in Nova Scotia. They soon came from around the globe to take the self-help message and methods home to their developing countries.

"People would write for information and they would arrive," said Sister Doyle. "At that time Antigonish seemed to be a place where you could do something. You could do it yourself and the people themselves could do it. That's why it attracted so many people."

Ever the unconventional, it seems Coady began to think locally and act globally. He was a study in contrasts. A big thinker in a small town.

A faithful priest and a radical revolutionary.

The international institute named in Coady's honour opened its doors shortly after this giant fell in 1959. But he had been a visionary. Coady's prediction back in the 1930s that a building called International House would one day stand on the St.F.X. campus came true.

Since it began, 'The Coady' has had over four thousand campus graduates and about twenty-two thousand overseas graduates. In 1999, students from twenty-one different countries came to the university town.

It's a joy to see the radical mix of peoples, the bemused expressions when they hear their first Scottish bagpipes, or the big smiling face of a new 'Coady' student asking, wide-eyed, "Is this snow?"

Dr. Moses Coady brought opposites together. He turned the world on its head, right here in our backyard.

Why is it Called Burnside?

The poetic genesis of an industrial park's name.

This story is dedicated to the youngest CBC Radio One listener who ever phoned in to the "Information Morning" answering machine with a question for me to research. He was polite and smart, with a name as big as his curiosity: Thomas Jefferson. I loved his call. His young voice, comically tiny for its bold confidence, left this message on the machine:

"Oh, hi. My name is Thomas and I'm four and a half. And I have a question for Mr. Know-It-All. And, umm, I'm four and a half. Why is it called 'Burnside'? Bye."

Ha! Here's a kid used to hearing my stories on Mom's radio from his car seat who obviously wondered about the name of that concrete jungle that Mom was driving through that day. The story behind the name follows below. Thanks Thomas!

It's the largest industrial park in the east. Burnside, the sprawling business site in the north end of Dartmouth, is bursting with more than a thousand companies, over fifteen thousand employees. Who would have guessed this concrete goliath took its name from a lovely freshwater stream?

The meek origin of the name of that heavily commercialized place—Burnside—can be found in an oil painting made in 1880. It's an idyllic scene of an old crofter-style house, surrounded by colourful trees, on a small hill that slopes down to a babbling brook. The painting in the Dartmouth Heritage Museum depicts the lovely hilltop house of Scottish pioneer Duncan Wadell. Using the Scottish word for stream—*burn*—he named his charming bungalow by the brook, "Burnside."

The name stuck for the surrounding Wadell lands and, later, for the mammoth 'business community'—as they like to call the industrial park—that now squats in full concrete and asphalt splendour where the beautiful burn once babbled.

The Wadell farmland, then prosperous with hay, cattle, and cranberry bogs is now home to such things as "THE GIANT WAREHOUSE CLEARANCE SALE—WHERE EVERYTHING MUST GO!"

It's sad. The price of progress. But the contrast gets sadder. Long after Mr. Wadell rented his farmhouse to tenant farmers, it became a barracks for soldiers during the war. The lovely slope was known as Ack-Ack Hill, a target practice site for the army, named for the sound of the guns. Still later, the army really moved in to capture the old Wadell lands. A dangerous military storage facility, Canadian Forces Ammunition Depot Bedford, now sits behind chain-link fencing on the edge of former Wadell property. Local commuters know the site as Magazine Hill.

The military magazine certainly ain't no babbling brook. I've toured the site. Concrete bunkers imbedded into hills house all our military's ammo for this half of Canada: bombs, torpedoes, bullets, mines, grenades, and so on.

So how did we get from there to here? From burn to bomb? From cottage to commerce? The transfer of the valuable Burnside land began with an odd clause in Mr. Wadell's will. It had to do with redheadedness, of all things!

Anita Price, the museum historian who showed me the painting, explained that "one of his grandsons had red hair as he (Mr. Wadell) did. So he left the Burnside property to the redheaded grandson specifically for that reason. He was also his namesake, a younger Duncan Wadell—Duncan Wadell Lynch."

An innocent infant inherited that land where now stand massive monuments to corporate capitalism and military might. Are you catching the irony here? Over generations, the rolling farm property was handed down and eventually sold off to various buyers.

A century-old map helped the historian locate the specific spot where the Wadell homestead stood. The site of the charming country house depicted in the idyllic painting is now the metal scrapyard of Sagadore Cranes and Equipment, on Windmill Road. No need for poetic stretches here to hammer home my point. The land ain't what it used to be.

But what of the burn itself? Beneath the industrialization and militarization, perhaps the symbolic stream still flows. Inspired by that thought, the historian and I got in my car one day to go on a stream search.

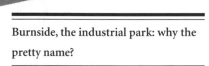

Burnside, the industrial park: why the pretty name?

We drove slowly down the tree-lined Wright's Cove Road, beside Sagadore Cranes, heading towards Halifax Harbour. It's a lovely, out-of-the-way road through pretty woods. It just happens to be on the fringe of one of Canada's largest commercial business communities, where you can buy anything from doughnuts to doorknobs by the gross.

I wanted to find the stream. I wanted even just a bit of burn to gurgle up out of the modern mire of our progress. I'm a sucker for symbolism.

And lo, what lay before us, betwixt the sparse trees? We stopped. Anita

Price looked from the car window. "Oh, there's something," she said.

It was a lush, soggy marshland area. The noise of traffic and industry wafted somewhere over those spruce. But at that spot was a beautiful boggy clearing, perhaps good for cranberry growing in another era. Anita got into the moment and pointed at something. "Not a fast-moving stream, but you can see some current down near the rocks."

And there it was! The burn of Mr. Wadell's Burnside. At least, I'd like to think it was. And the historian graciously left room for it to be true.

"Maybe *that's* his burn," she mused. "Maybe *that's* his burn."

Small World at Vimy Ridge

A twist of fate and family in the trenches.

I n 1917, a strange twist in history, a remarkable coincidence, occurred for a Nova Scotian soldier fighting in France at the infamous battle of Vimy Ridge. But it wasn't discovered until nearly sixty years later.

Gordon Rafuse of Berwick made the discovery after tracing his father's wartime footsteps.

By most accounts, Vimy was where Canada made its stand as a nation, amid mud, blood, guts, and gore. But Gordon's father, Henry Rafuse, wouldn't talk much about war, except to describe the trenches soldiers lived in. "How muddy they were and how many rats and lice and everything they had," said Gordon.

"Guys would get get sick and they'd get trench foot," said Gordon.

Henry Rafuse also told his son about "the Hellish noises when they were firing the guns."

One day a slim, small book called simply *The Seventh* was sent to the Rafuse home. It's a history of the #7 Canadian Siege Battery—Henry Rafuse's regiment. Another member of the group wrote it from the diaries and drawings made by the men in the Vimy trenches.

The book credits Henry Rafuse for saving his comrades' lives. In the heat of battle, there was a mistake during the loading of a big artillery gun. An explosive shell ended up in the wrong place.

Here's the historical account from the book: "The tray tilted and the shell fell out. The top of the 106 fuse being torn off and the shearing wire exposed as it hit the tail of the gun."

A dangerous explosive was at the group's feet, ready to blow!

The narrative continues: "With everyone looking on, Rafuse picked up the shell, unfused it and threw the fuse away. The acting bombardier who was in charge learned…later that six pounds pressure on the shearing wire would have detonated the shell and vaporized him and his crew if Rafuse had bungled the job. Fortunately Rafuse had a very sure pair of hands."

Nova Scotia's Henry Rafuse: defused a live shell at Vimy.

How about that? Perhaps he deserved a medal? But when Gordon brought it up, Henry Rafuse would hear none of it. "'What the Hell's the good of them?…' That's all I got for an answer," said Gordon.

That's the way his father, Henry, was.

"That's the way a lot of them were," said Gordon. "They weren't looking for glory. They just wanted to get that war over with and get back home."

Still, Gordon wanted to know more. In the 1970s, as a sergeant in the Canadian military himself, based in Germany, Gordon drove to France, to the ridge at Vimy.

With his slim history of his

father's regiment in hand, he paced the nicely manicured, green field where once men and horses were blasted to grisly fragments. Using the book's hand-drawn, numbered map of the Vimy Ridge trenches, he walked the site of the very slit trench where his Dad had survived through the hell of The Great War.

"Number 22 was the little dugout he was in, along with Gunner Davis." Gordon needed to see that place, to absorb the ghostly feeling of events long ago that shaped his father's life. "It was one of the best things I ever did and I was glad I was able to do it," he said.

He still holds boyhood memories of his father's late night screams erupting from nightmares of that war. That's why he sent his small history book of the #7 Canadian Siege and Battery to Canadian history writer Pierre Berton, who was preparing his book *Vimy*, published in 1986. Gordon wanted his father's regiment remembered, on the record. Henry Rafuse's story is told in the final pages of Berton's work.

It was a story Gordon had taken to heart that day in France, walking where his father had fought and survived, where thousands of Canadians perished.

"That was more than tingles," he admitted. "Such emotional feelings; I've only come across them in times when I was in a place that had a lot of history or in an ancestral place."

Oddly enough, Vimy was also an ancestral place to the Rafuse family. A strange family coincidence unfolded there, which Gordon discovered while overseas.

He learned about a German book that was a four-hundred-year history of his family name, Rafuse, or in German, Rehfuss. Other contacts lead him to 82-year-old Carl Rehfuss, a possible relative. He met with the old German and talked.

When Gordon mentioned his father and Vimy Ridge "that perked him up right away!"

"He said 'I was in the German army at the time. I was a lieutenant. I was at Vimy Ridge at the same time, so we were fighting against each other.'"

Later, using the four hundred year family history, Gordon determined Carl Rehfuss and Henry Rafuse were distant cousins! "I figured it was about 14 generations back that they came together," he said.

Fellow family members over time, they were firing at each other over the line. In war, they were of the same blood yet each was trying to shed the other's.

It was a family connection Gordon Rafuse never expected.

Sweet Inspiration

Nova Scotia's lyrical link to a classical Christmas composition.

"A Ceremony of Carols" is a long, beautiful, musical tradition performed during the holiday season by Christmas choirs the world over. But I wonder how many serious music lovers know of Nova Scotia's influence on its creation?

The 23-minute classical opus, an inspiring cycle of medieval and sixteenth-century poetry, is a modern-day musical celebration written by the top British composer of the twentieth century, Benjamin Britten.

His is a household name to fans of the classical music genre—as well-known as Britney Spears to a teenager, you might say! (If the pop star's star hasn't popped by the time this book is published, that is.)

As one of the world's leading talents in his day, Britten, not Britney, is remembered for his famous opera called "Peter Grimes."

His large body of work includes "The War Requiem," "Noah's Flood," and many more examples of brilliant musical craftsmanship. Britten's musical mind seemed boundless. He wrote, conducted, and performed. His impressive creations are treasured by musical archivists in England. His life story is detailed in a thick biography by Humphrey Carpenter.

All this is to say that Benjamin Britten was a big-time mover in music circles. And still is.

Each December, the high notes of Britten's "A Ceremony of Carols" soar to the ceiling arches of cathedrals and music halls in Halifax, in Britain, and further afield, angelic voices of children's choirs lifting its musical waves higher and higher, then crashing down to gentle softness. The dramatic composition opens and closes with a procession written for singers to enter and depart the stage in soft song, bearing lighted candles. Poetic lyrics sung in Old English by young, vaulting voices. It's stirring.

The story of how it was written is fascinating. In 1942, Britten was sailing in wartime waters on a neutral Swedish vessel, the *Axel Johnson*, from New York back to England. He was suffering from writer's block, or composer's block, at sea. The ship's crew was noisy; the voyage, dull. The war in his homeland preoccupied his mind. The music just wasn't coming to him. But his ship stopped over in Halifax for a few days.

While in Nova Scotia, Britten stumbled across something in Halifax that inspired him to compose "A Ceremony of Carols."

His biographer writes that the inspiration came from a book of poetry that Britten purchased at a bookstore in Halifax in 1942. That book restored Britten's musical muse. He began sketching out "A Ceremony Of Carols" on the voyage home. Perhaps he even started writing it in Halifax during his three- or four-day stopover. By the end of his ocean crossing, the composition was complete.

So, what was the magical book that broke Britten's composer's block and gave the world this marvelous music?

That's what I wondered.

Two local classical music lovers steered me in the right direction. Columnist Brian Flemming put me on to Colin May of Dartmouth. He knew about Britten's published letters, a volume that includes a post-card showing Halifax's Public Gardens, written during Britten's stay in Nova Scotia.

I found the two-volume set, *Letters from a Life*, at the Mount Saint Vincent University Library. A helpful reference librarian dug deep into its index to discover…Yes!…the actual title of the old Halifax book Britten bought, read, scratched notes in, and borrowed poems from to build his musical monument to peace and innocence. The book that inspired him was *The English Galaxy of Shorter Poems* by Gerald Bullett, published in 1939. We sold it to Britten and the rest is music history!

Now you probably want to know which Halifax bookstore sold it to Britten. Shheesh! You don't ask for much, do you? O.K., here goes.

We know that Britten's ship was docked for a few days at a Halifax pier in 1942. According to my helpful friend, genealogical genius Terry Punch and his massive collection of city directories, there was a handful of Halifax bookstores within easy walking distance of the harbour in that year. There was one called Connolly's Books on Spring Garden Road, but it apparently sold mostly Catholic literature. Britten was Anglican. He might have gone as far up as the Anglican Cathedral bookstore on College Street. But it's a bit out of the way.

He more likely found it closer to the harbour in The Bookroom, Canada's oldest bookstore. In 1942, the bookstore stood on Barrington Street facing Spring Garden Road, where the towering Maritime Centre is now, just down the street from the present Bookroom. Back then, that store was run by Ryerson Press, United Church Publishing, a likely place for a British composer to find such a British book.

That's my best guess.

What a story! The province with the city that had the store that sold the book that inspired the composer who wrote the music that touches hearts around the world at Christmas time.

A Tale of Two Tuppers

*Linking a past Prime Minister of Canada
and the King of Tupperware.*

In this tale of two Tuppers, we learn of the link between Sir Charles Tupper—premier of Nova Scotia and prime minister a century ago—and Earl Silas Tupper, creator of the handy food container, Tupperware.

No, I am not making this up. It's a Tupper truth, vacuum sealed for factual freshness.

You see, Charles Tupper contacted me from the great beyond, Vancouver. He's not the ghost of the long dead politician. He is the

great, great grandson of the same; a direct descendant of the distinguished Sir Charles Tupper, the premier who ushered Nova Scotia into
Confederation.

"Is it true", I asked, "that Sir Charles Tupper, the medical doctor
from Amherst, Premier of Nova Scotia from 1864 to 1867, Prime
Minister of Canada in 1896, knighted by Queen Victoria—was related
to the king of the great American plastics empire, Tupperware?"

I had heard that rumour somewhere in my travels and had stored it
away, frozen in time, keeping it fresh for future consumption. This was
my chance to pop the top on it and give it the old taste test.

"I think he's a cousin…of some sort," said Charles, waffling.

Intrigued, I started in slowly to learn more. First, he told me about
a memento of Sir Charles' that his own father had handed down to
him. "He gave me a pipe, carved in the likeness of Sir John A.
Macdonald and he told me that it belonged to my great, great grandfather," said the modern-day
Charles Tupper.

He seemed proud. With good
reason.

The historic Charlottetown
Conference on Confederation in
1864 began when then Premier
Tupper, by formal resolution in
our House of Assembly, called
for a conference on the issue of
Maritime union. When the
agenda changed to a national
union, he joined in. He even
delayed an 1867 provincial
election just long enough to get
Confederation passed provin-
cially.

Despite blowing smoke out of
John A. Macdonald's head with his
prime ministerial pipe, Charles

Sir Charles Tupper with son Charles H.
Tupper and grandson Charles Tupper Jr.:
Nova Scotia's link with Tupperware!

Tupper later served John A. federally as the minister who gave the unifying Canadian Pacific railway its charter.

The modern-day Vancouverite Tupper visited his ancestor's gravesite in Halifax's Saint John Cemetery in the summer of 2000. "I was touched," he said, "it was just a matter of seeing it and being there and something I could say to my children if I ever have them; it had that connection."

His Tupperness was evident but linking prime ministers to plastics he couldn't do!

But there's more than one way to link a Tupper. I thought one of the many American Tuppers in cyberspace could help. Tonnes of Tuppers have contributed their family trees to a two volume genealogy: *The Tupper Family in the United States and Canada—1631-1995*, by Gateway Press.

One contributor I reached by phone is another Charles Tupper: Lieutenant Colonel Charles Tupper, Chief Nurse at the 43rd Medical Operations Squadron at Pope Airforce Base in North Carolina.

No, I am not making this up.

His grandfather Frank Tupper lived in Truro. "I've heard about him (Sir Charles T.)since I was a child, from my grandfather," said Lt. Colonel Tupper. "It's interesting to have a bit of history like that in your family."

"My grandfather spoke of him in that, when he was about 16, he remembered polishing his boots when he (Sir Charles T.) would come to visit the family there in (Truro) Nova Scotia," he said.

Then, with his Tupper family chart in front of him, Lt.Col. Charles Tupper and I worked through the Tupper tree over the phone.

Both the political Tupper and the plastics Tupper came from a Captain Thomas Tupper who's father was first in America, landing at Sandwich Massachusetts in 1635. Captain Tupper had sons named Israel and Eliakim. Then, they had sons. Israel's son was Samuel, Eliakim's son was Eliakim Jr.

The tree tracing was narrowing. "So that means Samuel and Eliakim Jr. were first cousins?" I said.

"Correct," said the military Tupper.

Repeating names he had listed in descending order, I climbed down the Tupper tree.

"...and Silas and Charles were second cousins, and Silas Freeman and Rev. Charles were third cousins, so Ezra and Sir Charles were fourth cousins and—one, two, three—Earl Silas is a fourth cousin, three times removed from Sir Charles," I said.

That was it! The King of Tupperware and the Prime Minister of Canada were fourth cousins three times removed!

"That follows on my map too," said Lt.Col. Tupper. "That's pretty distant!"

Charles Tupper's Halifax home: Armdale.

Close enough for me.

As for Lt. Col. Charles Tupper in North Carolina, he is Sir Charles Tupper's first cousin, three times removed. He and the Vancouverite Charles Tupper are related to the two famous Tuppers and to each other.

Now, encouraged by all this Tupper-tracing, Charles and Charles are keeping in touch by email. They swap notes on the two historic Tuppers: One preserved our great Canadian nation, the other preserved our leftovers.

The Hermit

A philosophical recluse deep in Nova Scotia's woods.

"He's agile yet! I'd like to see a man 83 years old stand on his head but he's the only one around can do it!"

Lloyd Bogle walks ahead of me in his red checkered hunting jacket and ball cap. Crunching through frozen puddles and crusty snow, deep in the woods, he's taking me on this bright winter day to visit the peculiar old hermit of Colchester County. It's January 1999, a sunny morning in contrast to the cold, unforgiving month that led up to it.

"I get a charge out of him," says Lloyd. "It's amazing how he toughs her out."

The crunching continues beneath our feet as we wind between tall trees, their grey leafless branches splitting the winter sun. Green spruce wear shawls of snow. It's a lovely walk in the woods for us. Reaching the edge of a lake with no sign of civilization around it, we follow the trail as Lloyd knows it, to the left.

For twenty-five years Lloyd's been tramping out here to visit his isolated friend in the forest. He found him while snowmobiling, back when our winters filled the forest with snow. We are looking for the hermit's home.

It's a mile's hike from the end of the nearest logging road, seven miles from the nearest village, Earltown. We are north of Truro, about halfway to River John, tramping through the back country, close to the Colchester-Pictou County line.

The Hermit's home since World War Two.

We stop in the stillness. Sunk in the snow, in a small clearing in the trees and not far from the lake, I see a tiny log hut. No bigger than a garden shed, it has a smoking stovepipe on top. There's no door, just a single hinged window facing the lakeside. Wind chimes hanging over the window are tinkling. A pair of snowshoes hangs on the side of the hut. Bits of this and that lay all around on the ground: plastic buckets with lids, tin cans, some metal scraps, sticks of firewood. A large fallen tree leans against the hut, broken over its roof.

Lloyd calls hello. A muffled sound from inside. We sit on a log in the warming sun and wait. Lloyd says it's best to let the reclusive fellow take his time to warm up physically and to the fact that we're there. He doesn't see many people. An hour passes with Lloyd and I talking, our backs to the hut. Then the window swings open.

Out climbs Willard Kitchener MacDonald. Eighty-three years old, he's thin with a scraggily grey beard, matted hair, a black toque, filthy face, and a dirty winter coat that's been torn and sewn up with twine. He sits beside us on the log. His face and his big hands are brown with dirt.

But beneath the grime, I learn there's a gentle man: polite, soft-spoken with a healthy sense of humour. Kitchener has been living in these woods since 1942. Remarkably, he has survived 57 bitter Nova Scotia winters, even on those days that dipped down to minus twenty degrees, like it did just a few weeks earlier.

"I was thinkin' it's the coldest day I ever seen," he says about that day. "I didn't know what the temperature was though."

I ask him what he did on that frigid day.

"Oh I think I broke an axe handle and it's kind of bad weather to have a poor axe so I had to go to work and make a handle," he says, nonchalantly. "If you don't have no axe you're a gone goose."

He speaks casually about facing those harsh conditions, his voice raspy soft. His life out here is rough. Despite that, he still enjoys a joke. He offers me one he read in a magazine.

"An office worker slipped on some spilled coffee and broke his arm" said Kitchener, "and he now sports a sling which says 'Coffee Break!'"

With a slight smile he adds, "So, it kinda gets a person thinking, is it possible that coffee's not good for ya?"

I'm in the woods listening to *Reader's Digest* jokes from an eccentric hermit. It's strange. Because his situation here is not funny.

Having no axe would have meant no chopped wood for the self-made metal woodstove in his tiny hut. And hence, no heat. His hovel has no electricity, no hot water, no toilet. Just a dirt floor, a bench with a fur to sleep on and an old hubcap in which to fry his food on his crude stove. And in the corner, the World War Two Enfield rifle he once used to hunt deer.

The rifle was issued to him. He had it with him when he jumped from a troop train full of soldiers who were bound for Halifax and a ship heading overseas to war. Kitchener ran into these woods and has never left.

Lloyd's learned the story over the years. The train slowed for a junction, Kitchener jumped off and ran to hide in this forest he had known since his childhood. He wouldn't tell me why he did it. But he has told Lloyd that he knew that he wouldn't be able to take a human life. Instead, he gave up on his own life and spent it here, alone.

He gets his supplies in Earltown from the village general store: canned food, flour, old used books. In good weather he used to bicycle into town until his bike was stolen from the spot he kept it near the logging road. Now he walks in.

Lloyd and some others arranged for Kitchener to receive the old age pension. He refused to sign for it but it was approved anyway. The money is held in trust. The store owner dips into it to pay for Kitchener's goods.

Kitchener used to get regular cheques from the fund—spending money—but he never cashed them. He has no love nor need of the world's money.

In fact, the winter before, he lost a cheque in the wind while return-ing home on foot from his trip to town. He almost lost his life as well. A vicious winter storm had whipped up quickly. A raging wind erased the return trail under swirling gusts of snow. The temperature dropped. The old man of the woods was losing his way.

"It was getting dark," he says. "I had to hurry in order to get out of it. Finally I had to climb a tree. The snow was right up over my knees. Hard trompin'. And finally I noticed this clearing. I made a beeline for that quick as I could and I managed to reach it just in time. I managed to get in all right. I just got out by the skin of my teeth you might say."

Kitchener's dramatic dash into these woods, and that near-death storm experience, contrast sharply with his long life of mostly monoto-nous days and slowly passing years. He reflects on life with a mix of melancholy and wonder. He's read the Bible cover to cover. He looks for answers in his favorite *Reader's Digest* articles.

"Oh mostly scientific stuff about other worlds and planets and stuff," he says.

"Why are you interested in that?" I ask.

"Well most everyone is, you know, that sort of thing."

I found myself agreeing.

"You know, you wonder if there's going to be another life after this one or something like that," he says. "Yes...or no. What do you think?"

"I'm confused about that myself," I say.

"Hmmm, so am I," he says. "I guess it just has to be for some reason."

This is not the blissful, Henry David Thoreau, Walden Pond experience he is living. I see that now. This old hermit is as lost as we all are about life. But he bears it completely alone, with absolutely no comforts.

"It says in one article I read that genius is born in solitude," he says. "I experiment with things like that, you know."

"What does solitude do for you?" I ask.

"Makes you feel funny. Also gives you nightmares, all alone, wondering about the world and all this stuff."

I feel suddenly sorry for him. But I tell myself he's here by choice. He's thoughtful, even philosophical, but he's got to be tough as nails too. I realize I'm intrigued not so much by his way but by his will. I'm looking at an absolute incarnation of stubborn determination in sooty clothes. Why does he live this way?

The Hermit in his hut: alone for almost 60 years.

He knows the war is over. I don't know why he's still here. I don't think he knows. His mind is confused. He just can't see beyond his one-day-at-a-time way of existing. He chooses to stick with the familiar.

He's been offered help. A new comfortable cabin—with a real wood stove, a kitchen, and a water pump—was built for him up the road. He refused to move in. I wonder if he feels he's running away from the world, or if he feels he doesn't deserve the world's offerings since he turned his back on its wartime service. We'll never know. He's just here. Not asking for anything and not willing to change. Noble and stubborn. Kitchener's chosen way of life just…is. And that seems to be all this odd man of the woods wants.

I'm not sorry for him. He could have worldly comforts but he's turned them down. I can't understand how he survives but I think I admire that he does.

He allows me to climb inside his dirty hut. The air is full of dust. The ceiling is low. I'm unable to stand. Kitchener pokes at a small fire in the tin box and then picks up a grimy, broken guitar. He plays in a style as unique as he is. His strumming is rough but rhythmic with a bit of a Spanish flamenco sound to it. But his tune repeats, coming around in circles to the beginning and starting again like an old record on a turntable. He's probably been playing the same tune for half a century. And will continue playing it.

When I ask him how long he plans to live out here he quotes a lyric from an old song:

"Push on to the end of the road," he says.

I understand. That seems to be his only plan. Kitchener lives just for each moment, like this one with his guitar in hand, his head back, eyes closed, and his music, awkward and a little sad.

Great Grave Digging Monks!

The secret remains of monastery's would-be saint.

A ncient religious rites. A rustic, remote monastery. Foreign gravediggers seeking holy remains in a secret crypt. Sure, it could be a medieval mystery novel but no—it's part of parish history in Tracadie, Antigonish County.

The parish includes the village of Monastery, named for its 175-year-old Catholic monastery in the woods. Picture tall, old, brick buildings with fanciful towers around a courtyard, a beautiful stained-glass chapel, a winding gravel road, farming fields, a serene shrine amongst the trees by a babbling stream. It's all still there.

In October 2000, a new group of monks moved into Our Lady of Grace Monastery, the fourth influx of monks since the French Trappists founded the place in 1825. But a modern mystery once surrounded its founder's buried remains.

Father Vincent de Paul Merle, a French Catholic Monk, arrived here by accident but was later considered for sainthood for his work. The order he belonged to tried and failed to establish itself in several American locations: Baltimore, Pennsylvania, Maryland, and New York. Called back to France in 1815, they set sail.

Stopping over in Halifax, they awaited good winds for overseas sailing.

Father Gabriel Bertoniere, a present-day Trappist now writing the history of his order in North America, told me from his monastic home in Spencer, Massachusetts, "Vincent left the boat for supplies. He made some purchases on land, not taking anything with him except his breviary, his prayer book."

Father Vincent returned to the Halifax pier "only to find that the wind had come up and and the captain had set sail. So there he was, stranded!"

Ironically, a Halifax priest named Father Burke had been plotting to attract monks here to serve the Mi'kmaq populations. Was Vincent's missing the boat divine influence? Some said so.

He stayed and almost settled at Chezzetcook, on Nova Scotia's Eastern Shore.

But his monastery was eventually created near the Antigonish County French communities of Pomquet, Tracadie, and Havre Boucher.

His start-up was humble. He founded a small female order of nuns called Trappestines whose convent was a few miles down the road from the present-day monastery. The men's monastery struggled.

Dedicated and resilient, Vincent "had lived through revolutionary times in France and was imprisoned on one occasion."

"He had a great love for common folk," said Father Gabriel. "Always happy to help out in a parish situation," he was "pastor in Tracadie on a number of occasions."

But as a founder, Father Vincent suffered from a "lack of organizational qualities."

His humble group grew to just six men, some Nova Scotians. After twenty difficult years, his monastery ultimately failed. But his loving way with the local people was—and is still—much honoured. He died in 1853.

More Trappists arrived and the monastery lived an ill-fated life, including two devastating fires, until 1900. The monks pulled up stakes. They reburied the remains of the monastery's founder, Father Vincent, in front of St. Peter's Church in Tracadie, and resettled in the U.S.

"These French monks, inspired by the local people, considered his canonization (elevation to saint) as a possibility," said Father Gabriel. "There was great desire."

The bishop approved it. That was step one. But with difficulty gathering necessary evidence for the long process in Rome, the drive to canonize Father Vincent was eventually dropped.

About 12-15 years ago, the modern-day Trappists in Massachusetts came to Tracadie hoping to reclaim Father Vincent's two-hundred-year-old remains from the grave at the Tracadie Church, to take them to the United States.

Lloyd Boucher, a local history buff in East Tracadie, remembers when the American monks arrived.

"They had a machine there digging for two days," he told me by

The monastery at Monastery: founded by a secret saint?

phone from his home, "but it wasn't in the right spot."

They couldn't find the founder's bones!

The gravemarkers had been removed years earlier. And Boucher wasn't about to help. "I knew where the grave was but they didn't," he said.

He has an old photo of the graveyard with the markers in place, showing where Father Vincent was buried. But he didn't let on. He was upset that a previous pastor had removed Father Vincent's gravestone and that the American monks had "trundled it off to their monastery in Massachusetts."

"They weren't going to take his remains too!"

Mr. Boucher was proudly defending a relic of his parish history. Today, permanently protected from digging monks, the grave is an officially designated heritage site.

At the old monastery, the Augustinians, another group of European monks who arrived after fleeing the Nazis in the 1930s, moved out just last fall. An orthodox Catholic order, the Maronites, are now taking the monastery at Monastery into its third century.

Cocktails and Confederation

The boozy birth of a nation in our own backyard.

T he birthplace of Canada! The cradle of Confederation! We've all heard about Charlottetown's claim to fame but how about Halifax—the nursery of Confederation? Oh yeah, perhaps the babe was born on the island but Nova Scotia was first to nurture our neonatal nation. But it wasn't nurtured on mother's milk, it was suckled on booze.

First, our esteemed Confederation fathers indulged heavily in champagne over in Green Gables Land. The visiting delegates from the Canadas—upper and lower, or Canada East and Canada West— brought today's equivalent of thirteen thousand dollars worth of bubbly to the island meeting.

Gone was the idea of maritime union that initially brought the maritime delegates together. A whole new nation loomed in those well-watered discussions.

George Brown, a delegate from Upper Canada, wrote of the 1864 Charlottetown conference to his wife: "…whether, as a result of our elegance, or the goodness of our champagne, the ice became completely broken, the tongues of the delegates wagged merrily…and the union was thereupon formally completed and proclaimed."

Then our founding fathers took their idea of nationhood on the road. Or, on the sea. First stop in spin-doctoring the message was Nova Scotia.

Sailing from PEI over to Pictou, upper and lower Canadian delegates toured the town. Some caught a stagecoach to our capital, while John A. Macdonald and others sailed on their steamer around to Halifax Harbour.

The partying continued.

Dr. Peter Waite, author of *The Life and Times of Confederation*, described that scene for me recently in Halifax: "They held informal discussions; did a lot of partying," he said. "They were making popular what had already been tentatively agreed to in Charlottetown."

Their socializing took the form of "great massive Victorian entertainment that ran seven to ten courses with speeches that lasted five hours so you really needed massive amounts of liquid."

One big dinner was held at the Halifax Hotel on Hollis Street, just south of Province House. *The British Colonist* newspaper printed John A. Macdonald's rousing speech:

"Sir, this meeting in Halifax will be ever-remembered in the history of British America; for here the delegates from the several provinces had the first opportunity of expressing their sentiments—we have been

The proud fathers of Confederation broke their news in Nova Scotia first.

unable to announce them before, but now let me say that we have arrived unanimously at the opinion that the union of the provinces is for the advantage of all…"

So, they said it here first! Baby's first public utterance.

But poor Joseph Howe was a bit too free with his speech. At a previous, similar gathering with equal amounts of hype and hooch, he openly praised Confederation. Oops! He forgot he was opposed.

A few months later he blamed the booze and revelry for his slip of the lip. Or you might say he found the terms of the agreement sobering. "He came out with a blistering attack (on Confederation) in January of 1865," said Waite.

Howe fought Confederation all the way to London, England. But approval was eventually granted by the Crown. Howe had no more options and was afraid opponents of the deal might turn to taking up arms. So, with time, Howe cautiously sidled up to the plan.

He didn't like the way Premier Tupper pushed it through the legislature though. "Rushed through at black midnight" was how Howe described Tupper's tactics.

Waite told me Joe Howe was caught in a tight spot. "He probably had to choose between leading a real resistance—almost take up rifles—or knuckling under to the British government," said Waite. After all, "Nova Scotia had technically agreed to it."

Canada's birth certificate was finally formally signed in Quebec City in 1867.

But Nova Scotia had almost turned away from that difficult delivery. Just after the Confederation deal was signed and sealed, a Nova Scotian election was held. A large majority of anti-confederate members were voted in, too late to abort the birth.

So the labour room delivery of our new-born country was due to two things: The timing of the vote and the raising of the wrist!

Running on Rum!

The religion, politics and business of booze in Nova Scotia.

R um is a word that sounds like you're drinking it. Beginning with a hungry growl sound, it dips pleasingly low then quickly up, ending pleasurably with a satiated 'Mmmmmm' sound. Perfectly onomatopoeic, the word is as intoxicating as the drink. Hence it brings its notoriety to expressions common in Nova Scotia's past: "the devil rum," "a tot of rum," "rum running." It's a word. It's a drink. And in our past—for good or for worse—it was a way of life. Pull up a stool, I'll pour you a shot of rum history.

Going back two hundred years, the navy's daily tradition of the tot of rum helped build community aboard the rocky, barnacled tall ships that cruised the seas for the Crown. Picture a tub of rum. Stay focused, now. Picture a line of sweaty, weary sailors, each given a wee copper pitcher full of their daily rum ration at sea. Centuries ago each received a half pint per day. That didn't work too well. Serving that much rum 'neat' could cause the ship to be 'on the rocks.' So, later came the two and a half ounce tot, or one half gill of rum.

This nautical tradition was not indulgent. At the Maritime Command Museum in Halifax I learned that rum was very practical at sea. It wouldn't grow skanky in its wooden barrels like drinking water would on a long voyage. Yeah, that's the reason sailors drank rum. It was better for them. Here's to good health! But leave it to the boss to carry a good thing too far. Admiral Vernon came along. His nickname, 'Old Grogram,' came from the name of the coarse fabric in his heavy cloak. The cheap admiral began watering down the Royal Navy's rum. You may still occasionally hear a bartender refer to a glass of 'Grog,' the name given Old Grogram's watery creation.

When Halifax took its newborn breaths as a neophyte garrison town

251 years ago, rum was there. Happy birthday, have a drink. In 1751 one of the first industries in Cornwallis's community was a distillery. First things first, I suppose. I would have hoped they'd at least drive the posts for the palisades before brewing booze. (It's not safe to drink and drive.)

Three years later, business was brisk. An ad in the *Halifax Gazette*, March 16, 1754, declares, "Choice Nova Scotia RUM to be sold by Joshua Mauger, at Two Shillings a Gallon, in any quantities not less than a Barrel."

Like an evolving creature, the devil's rum had crept ashore from the seagoing vessels onto 'dry' land. Then it became a dominating dinosaur crushing all in sight. Perhaps a flood analogy is more fitting. By 1849, the citadel town was awash in the demon liquid. There were four distilleries at work.

One critic wrote in an 1862 Presbyterian newspaper that the Nova Scotian capital was, "nothing less than a great big rumshop! Rum on the right hand, rum on the left; rum before you, rum behind you and rum all around you."

A lucrative liquid, rum ran the place. You were either a drinker or a seller. In their book *Tempered by Rum; Rum in the History of the Maritime Provinces*, Morrison and Moreira write of one early, eager Haligonian named George Hick, who abandoned his blacksmith trade to become a rum seller.

The year the city was founded Hick wrote to his wife in England, "I sell rum by the quart, and in smaller quantities. I buy it at 3s. a gallon, and lays out two guineas a week in it, by which I find I get money very fast…"

That fast money flowed further into the economy of the province as a whole. Settlers were given government incentives of three-and-a-half gallons of rum per head. Just for being here! Free rum and all the fish you could catch! Not a bad deal. In tough times, settlers found the rum trade easily bettered the fish market. Rum made fast money and was sometimes used as money—liquid currency. Some loggers and sawmill workers were paid in rum.

It wasn't just for social occasions anymore. Booze was business. It was also blood money. Tragically, rum was used as an incentive payment during the expulsion of the Acadians in 1755. Soldiers ordered to burn French homes were permitted to keep whatever rum they found. A dark time for dark rum.

Our boat builders benefited from rum, once the American prohibition hit. We no longer shipped just odd-shaped blue potatoes to Boston (the likely reason we were called Bluenoses), we shipped booze (Booze Noses?). Rum running brought excitement, good money and great stories to tell the grandchildren. A new rum-running boat design came out of it: low to the water with no masts to avoid detection by the American Coast guard.

The writer Harry Bruce records that the smugglers picked up liquor often at St. Pierre and Miquelon. Then they'd sail it south to the American coast, anchor offshore, meet an accomplice vessel, and make the deal. Some Bluenose rum runners delivered right to the American shoreline.

Of course the Excited Snakes of America wasn't dry alone. Halifax dried up before World War One ended. The province voted for temperance a few years later. That's when all the fun started. Despite temperance hall meetings and preachers and lawmakers demanding alcoholic abstinence, fun was being had. Where alcohol was still permitted for medicinal reasons, doctor's prescriptions for spirits were churned out in bulk, especially at holiday times. Must have been some nasty bug going around every Christmas.

Bootlegging and rum running became a deeply rooted tradition.

I know a former RCMP rum patroller, now in his 90s, who recalls combing the coves of our coast in search of criminal rum dealers. That was a long time ago. Prohibition ended here in 1930. That same RCMP patroller told me that years later he worked for a certain political party that paid campaign funds for cases of the classic Demerara Rum. A pint for a vote was the deal in the northeastern end of the province in the 1950s. I'm not sure what it was on the southern or western shore. It was of course just part of our ever-developing democracy—a simple reward for voters showing up to exercise their franchise. (And their elbows.)

Booze for votes today? Nah, not anymore. Well, probably not. Not often anyway. Maybe only every, well…four years, if that.

The spirit of those illegal spirits of prohibition lives on in occasional secret stills you hear about from time to time. I met a retired coal miner in Cape Breton who left the mine and now tends his shine—from mine dark to moonshine. His product is a clear, dangerous looking liquid, clear like one-hundred-proof vodka or like colourless kerosene. In fact that's about how powerful it tastes. A nice refreshing beverage! He and his friends have been drinking it safely for years.

For all the demon drink's distasteful faults, these spirits were useful in their own way. They boosted our economy, brought out the vote, drew the faithful together, and steeled the nerves of hard-working sailors.

I remember interviewing a Sambro swordfisherman, Harold Henneberry, whose boat went down three hundred miles off Newfoundland. He and the crew had mere minutes to throw a few necessary things into rowboats and escape. Among compass, drinking water, blanket, and oars, the men grabbed up eleven bottles of warmth and comfort for the marathon row back to shore. They made it. It took seven miserable days. They gave their one remaining bottle to the first fisherman who met them in the cove.

Saving Private Searle

A wartime Bible finds its way home from Vimy Ridge.

T he Bible in Duncan Searle's hand is not a stereotypically thick and formidable tome. This 'Good Book' is small, plain brown, and pocket sized; a wartime Bible. It belonged to Duncan's grandfather, a lucky survivor of the brutal Vimy Ridge battle of World War One. Apparently they were standard issues to many Canadian soldiers: The Word of the Lord writ small to carry into an enormous maelstrom of death and danger. A bit of Heaven in Hell.

Sitting in his home away from home, watching the peaceful North-umberland Strait shoreline, Duncan sips his coffee and tells me a Bible story—*this* Bible's story. He explains that it wasn't just a Holy Book to his grandfather, it was his war diary too. And it survived a sort of mystical journey home to the Searle family, eighty years after its owner almost didn't make it home.

Duncan is a teacher in the town of Truro. He cherishes this little brown Holy Book because of the scrawled pencil marks inside the cover. They're his grandfather's chronicle of battles leading up to the bloodbath of Vimy Ridge.

Private John James Searle—Jack to his buddies—was originally in the 193rd Battalion which was broken up and dispersed to other units. Regimental number 901335, Jack Searle was with the 85th at Vimy, living through war stories a young Duncan would later absorb while growing up. But with this little Bible in his hands, those stories hit home with greater force. Duncan opens the cover of the thin hardcover book. There's a printed inscription that reads, "Be strong and have good courage."

He casually reads his grandfather Jack's wartime scribbles.

"Bombardment on Vimy Ridge, Mar 26 1917," he reads. "It said 'biggest' bombardment, and then the 'biggest' is scratched out because there's another line saying 'biggest bombardment on Vimy Ridge April 9, 1917.'"

Private Jack Searle's next diary entry in the Bible has the shock of contrast. He noted the day: a day symbolic of peace, that would become infamous as a day of death.

"It says, 'Easter Monday Morning, 5:30 O'clock.'" Duncan thinks he recalls that Easter Monday was the day our men went over the top at Vimy Ridge. And so it was; April 9, 1917. The scene was horrendous—a battlefield of death on a day of rebirth.

In his book *Spearhead to Victory: Canada and the Great War*, war historian Daniel G. Dancocks collected an eye-witness account of the first day of the Vimy Ridge battle on Easter Monday morning:

"At 5:30, a canopy of shrieking steel exploded over their heads…'The deafening roar of the guns and the trench mortars, the chattering of machine guns, the swishing, rushing sounds of shells followed by crunching explosions produced a combination of noise that was almost overwhelming.' Then the troops…were on their feet and slogging up the slopes."

That was the horror of Vimy. Private Jack Searle of Truro was among those men slogging through that godforsaken chaos with his Holy Book-diary tucked in his heavy pack. Artillery fire punctured the sky. Our infantry pushed forward through barbed wire and muddy trenches. Driving wind, snow, and sleet mixed with the hailstorm of German bullets flying at them.

So what about Private Searle? Was he saved or was he killed? Duncan reads on. "The next entry in the back of the book, in pencil again, says 'Landed in Blitey, April.'"

He was suddenly in England! My puzzled look asks the obvious question.

"My grandfather was wounded," Duncan explains. "Shot in the head, shot in the leg, and he was gassed. So they sent him back to England to patch him up in hospital."

That was one very lucky, though very injured, young soldier. Truro's Private Jack Searle lived to tell this tragic tale with a happy ending. But that wasn't quite where it ended, and it wasn't all tragic. Not the way Duncan tells it. He just has to chuckle at his grandfather's misfortune, and his fortune of near-misses. You see, after coming out of that muddy, bloody mess alive, Private Searle was shipped home at an unfortunate time, to recover in hospital in Halifax. It was soon December 1917.

Lying bandaged and weak with several other wounded soldiers in his hospital room, Jack Searle's world was rocked again.

"He was in hospital just in time to survive the next big catastrophe in Canadian history, which was the Halifax explosion!" said Duncan, amused.

The windows of the hospital room were shattered. The room itself, destroyed. All the men recovering there were killed by the blast. All except one.

"My grandfather survived that," said Duncan, shaking his head. "Although they didn't find him until the latter part of the afternoon!

They dug him out. And he was still trying to get over the mustard gas and his head wound and his leg wound!"

You tell me, was he lucky or unlucky? Either way, he narrowly escaped death more than once. Something kept him alive. Something.

The unstoppable private's zest for life was quite undiminished as Act Three of this tragic comedy unfolds. With his hospital room in shambles, the injured young soldier was packed up and put on a train, bound for the comforts of the hospital in Truro. But it was filled to capacity. As Duncan tells it, even schools were made into makeshift hospitals, and every physician from miles around was there.

"The hospital didn't have any place for him."

Private Searle's wife, Duncan's grandmother, came to the train station by horse and buggy to pick him up. She took the patient home to nurse his wounds in his own bed. At this point, Duncan's eyes twinkle at me. He laughs and then spills the punchline.

"He had survived the Halifax explosion. He survived Vimy Ridge. His head was shot. His leg was wounded. And his lungs were shot with the mustard gas."

What's so funny about that?

"Nine months after that my father was born! So he was wounded," Duncan chortles, "but he wasn't damaged!"

Ha! Private Searle had clearly begun the healing process!

But, not to be crude, Duncan ends this war Bible story on that note for a reason. Renewal, regeneration, procreation and lineage; these thoughts flow into his mind as he weighs those near-misses in his grandfather's lucky life. That's why Duncan is here to tell the tale. Had the bullet entered a little to the left perhaps, or had the hospital bed been a bit closer to the raining glass shards from the exploding windows, maybe Duncan wouldn't be here. Twists of fate, moments in time make a life. It's like the mysterious way the little Bible came to be in Duncan's hands in the first place—another bit of mystical chance.

Duncan had taken a phone call one day from a man who asked if he was related to John James Searle. It took a moment for him to recognize his own grandfather's full formal name. The caller, George Manley of South Maitland, said he had a small military Bible with that name on it.

The World War Two veteran had seen the small Bible at an auction. His uncle had also fought at Vimy so Mr. Manley bought the book for two dollars. Knowing there were Searles in the Truro area, Mr. Manley began calling every Searle in the phone book until he reached Duncan.

He told me he felt compelled to search for the Searle family who owned the Bible. He knew it would have meaning for them. Duncan didn't even know it existed. He grew curious. The teacher took his 13 year old son, three generations removed from the soldier Searle, to visit Mr. Manley and retrieve the Good Book.

The veteran and the teacher talked for three hours of war battles and moments in time lived long ago. The young lad listened intently, lapping up these tales of his great grandfather's war experience. Tales he hadn't heard his father mention much before. But seeing his grandfather's scribbled notes in that Bible made Duncan realize more fervently the family heritage he has.

George Manley understood. You see, his uncle and namesake, who fought at Vimy, was also in the 193rd Battalion with Jack Searle before it was broken up! He went to the 25th, another battalion at Vimy. So George Manley's uncle had been there, somewhere, as Private Jack Searle sat in a muddy trench making hasty notes in the back of his Bible which George Manley had purchased some eighty years later and returned to the Searles. Imagine!

Fate and families. Twists in time. Why and how do such things happen so often, so profoundly, in this little province on the continent's edge?

Looking across the ocean waves, Duncan Searle mused about that strange confluence of coincidence. It had meaning for him.

"It's like this Bible all of a sudden popped up, you know, forty-five years after my grandfather died, and was delivered to me. There's something mystical about that," he said.

The timing was important for him too.

"It has an effect on you. I'm forty-eight. You start to think about who you are and where you come from. It's amazing how things pop up to just sort of tweak you on the way a bit."

Yes, it is amazing.

Dirt Cheap and Scot Free (Or is it Free Dirt and Cheap Scots?)

Why a plot of Nova Scotian ground sits for ceremony in Scotland.

High on the grand hilltop perch of Edinburgh Castle, the old and New Scotland are bonded by…dirt. It is officially-declared Nova Scotian dirt. The story goes that a plot of Nova Scotian earth, sanctioned centuries ago by Scotland's king, comprises part of the ground once covered by the Esplanade approach to the historic castle. I walked on that spot once and didn't even know I was really on my home turf!

This special plot of land was reserved for the ceremonious granting of titles to members of a unique order of noblemen: Men who all wanted to own a piece of Nova Scotia without ever coming here. No, not German millionaires.

Here's how it happened. Back when Scotland was sharing, rather than retreating from England's power base, Scotland agreed to share her king, James VI. In 1603, he accepted the English crown as well and became James I of England. He did dual duty as monarch. The double crown fit and he shared its influence with his fellow Scot and close associate—the poet, philosopher, and active Mason Sir William Alexander.

Sir Willy was the first great Nova Scotia promoter. But really it was his son Sir Willy Junior who did the dirty work. He sailed over and settled in Port Royal on July 28, 1629. But it was Sir Willy Senior—the mastermind of New Scotland—who gave us our flag and coat of arms. And we thank him for that.

This erudite gentleman also gave this rugged chunk of coastline its scholarly Latin name, Nova Scotia. (No, it ain't Gaelic.) Sir Willy, as I like to call our founder, and King James formally bestowed the fanciful title of Knight Baronet of Nova Scotia on anyone with money to invest in this homeland away from home.

The Baronets of Nova Scotia purchased large pieces of land here and they took possession of it over there. It was like signing a real estate deal in the agent's office, without ever seeing the property. The Baronet would stand on that special Nova Scotian plot of soil and take "sasine," or possession, of his title and his distant land. And, in return, the crown would take possession of the new Baronet's coins. It cost three thousand merks. I'm not sure of the exchange rate on a merk, today.

The first three title buyers were dubbed Baronets of Nova Scotia in 1625. According to *The Scotsman in Canada*, Vol.I by Wilfred Campbell, L.L.D., the premier baronet, Sir Robert Gordon, received sixteen thousand acres of Nova Scotia!

At the time, Nova Scotia was part of the independent Kingdom of Scotland. So the land grants were ratified and confirmed in the Parliament of Scotland at Edinburgh. By the time Scotland and England joined in royal union in 1707, there had been over a hundred baronetcies created.

Jim St. Clair, a Cape Breton historian, is descended from the only baronet to actually come all the way over here to visit his plot of land. Lord Ochiltree settled his group at Baleine, on the island.

The retired University College of Cape Breton professor told me the baronet scheme failed when a later king, Charles, traded all the New Scotland land to France for love and for money.

"He wanted to gain the dowry of his wife who was French," said Jim. "He felt that a purse in the hand was worth all these acres in the wilderness of North America."

So the whole baronet program became folly. It failed. It did not increase colonization much. Ochiltree, the only baronet to settle on our shores, was wiped out by the French. The title never had any power. And King Charles gave away the whole works anyway. Though some say that was not his intention, it just worked out that way in the give and take of state negotiations.

Worse yet, the plot of Nova Scotian soil in Scotland may also be fake! Left with the impression that actual soil from here was ceremoniously shipped to Scotland by king's order, I learned differently.

Premier Angus L. Macdonald, a fervent Cape Breton Scot, understood that the king had simply designated a plot of castle ground as Nova Scotian, for the sake of the baronet ceremonies.

That's why the *Mail Star* reported on Oct. 21, 1953 that our premier visited Edinburgh castle to correct a "fiction." Macdonald sprinkled some of our dirt on the Edinburgh Castle grounds and made a speech. "Nova Scotia, more than three hundred years ago, was annexed to Scotland by a fiction," he said. "Let me complete the task today by depositing a handful of Nova Scotia earth."

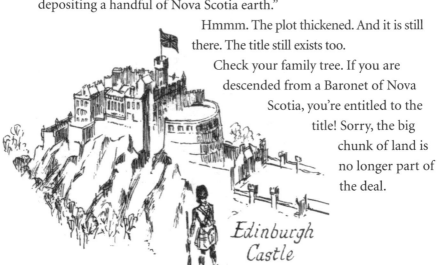

Hmmm. The plot thickened. And it is still there. The title still exists too.

Check your family tree. If you are descended from a Baronet of Nova Scotia, you're entitled to the title! Sorry, the big chunk of land is no longer part of the deal.

Edinburgh Castle

Nova Scotia: Captain Cook's Drawing Board

The famous chartmaker began his international map making on our shores!

A t the helm of his ship, Captain James Cook's mission was to boldly go where no man had gone before. History marks him as a great world explorer and expert nautical chart maker of the mid-1700s. His sharp technical skills, still evident in modern navigation charts, were honed and perfected right here in Nova Scotia! He arrived in eastern Canada as a young British ship's master and left as King's Surveyor, a father of the early science of hydrography.

After getting his start on our shores, Cook set sail on the world stage. He spent his life exploring, discovering, surveying, and drawing nautical charts and maps of exotic places barely touched if at all by white, European influence: Antarctica, Tahiti (before Captain Bligh), New Zealand, Australia, even up the northwest coast of North America. He tried to find the Northwest Passage over top of Canada in very early days.

Cook's work was even respected by Britain's enemies of the day: the Americans and the French. "So much so that they ordered their ships not to interfere with him," said Derrick Haggerston, a former publicity person for the English port town of Whitby, the origin of Cook's voyages.

"Even they recognized the

Halifax monument to Captain Cook: he sharpened his pencils here.

standards of his work; he was the best there ever was," he said to me from his home in North Vancouver.

And that "best ever" began here.

Years before Captain Cook made his famous South Pacific voyages, he came to Nova Scotia as a young ship's master under Captain Simcoe of the Royal Navy ship *Pembroke*. Cook was even at the fall of Louisbourg in 1758. I know! Who knew?

Cook's biographer, J.C. Beaglehole, describes in *The Life of Captain James Cook* how Cook stepped ashore at Kennington Cove, Cape Breton. He was curious to see there a man using a new land-surveying device, a small portable table on a tripod. The man squinted along the top of it in various directions and made notes.

The man was Samuel Holland, a Dutch military surveyor under James Wolfe. Meeting Holland changed Cook's life. "He taught Cook quite a bit about the art of surveying from the perspective of a land surveyor," said Darrell Burke, Heritage Interpreter with the Maritime Museum of the Atlantic, in Halifax.

"Cook combined that with his experience as a sailing master, navigator and, using those techniques, elevated hydrography—chartmaking—from an art form to a more precise science."

In Louisbourg Harbour, then later in Halifax Harbour, Cook and Captain Simcoe regularly welcomed the surveyor Samuel Holland aboard the *Pembroke* for chartmaking sessions during the winters. Holland became one of Cook's tutors, as did surveyor Lieutenant J.F.W. Desbarres. So Captain Cook was trained here!

He and his tutors charted Halifax Harbour and worked on surveys of our coastline. Not only that, they were also working "to update or create charts of the the the St. Lawrence and the Gulf which the British fleet later used during the invasion of Quebec."

Yes, a tool of attack on French Canada was drafted here. Charts drawn in Halifax brought General Wolfe's troops safely to Quebec's shores and the Plains of Abraham in 1759. The battle there sealed the fate of French power in Canada. So Cook gave us that historic link with the birth of our nation.

With the end of the Seven Years War in 1763, Cook was appointed

King's Surveyor. He spent some years charting the coast of Newfoundland, using the new method he learned here, incorporating land surveying with coastal surveying. Cook would leave his heaving vessel, set up instruments on a high point of land and triangulate from the hill down to shoreline and out to his anchored ship, for greater accuracy in his measurements.

Around Newfoundland, he also used a small, specially converted ship called the *Grenville*—probably the first ever hydrographic vessel—for his work out of Halifax.

Halifax remembers Captain James Cook with a federal historic monument. It's up on Fort Needham Hill, beside the Halifax Explosion memorial bell's tower. A stone cairn faces the harbour where Captain Cook spent those winters 240 years ago learning charting techniques which, the plaque acknowledges, he later adapted and "put to such good use in Newfoundland and the South Pacific."

He learned it here first!

A Hitchhiker's Guide to Genealogy

An Acadian hero's homeward travels and twisted roots.

"Headin' home?"

I knew where the easy-going young hitchhiker was headed before I asked. He had that look: standing by the outbound exit from Halifax, shouldering a red knapsack, on a clear, cool Friday of a Thanksgiving weekend. It was written all over his pleasant, placid face. He was getting out of the city. Probably home for Mom's cooking. I've been there. I knew that look. So I pulled over and picked him up. I felt no risk since the last time I rescued a highway hitcher we talked until we learned we were related through my mother's cousins. That can happen here. I thought I would learn this humble thumber's story too.

Everyone has one, and I collect them. Boy, did he have one! As I drove, he told me a remarkable true story of family and of home and of the powerful pull of this small province that draws the one to the other.

But before he even spoke, I foreshadowed that sense of small-worldness with my sudden realization, "We've met before!" Leonard Gaudet knitted his thick eyebrows at me, then smiled. He was the same home-bound hiker I had picked up, on the same long weekend, exactly one year before! True story. Only in Nova Scotia! Leonard was heading to Pictou for a decent Thanksgiving meal, as I had guessed.

This fateful fluke was a perfect start to his twisted tale of travel, family and odd encounters. Leonard's family story dates back to a hero of the great Acadian expulsion in 1755.

While we zoomed along the empty asphalt, Leonard pulled a thick sheaf from his knapsack: his complete genealogy going back eight generations. He was taking all his relatives home for the weekend. Proof in hand, Leonard began to update me on his research. Since last we talked, a year previous, Leonard had reached back an eighth generation to the great Jacques Maurice Vigneau. He was an unsung hero to the desperate, dispersed French Acadians in the mid-1700s.

Jacques Maurice was a courageous and skilled negotiator and merchant. He had singlehandedly bargained for passage of a hundred expelled Acadians, back up the American eastern seaboard, toward their British-dominated home province, Nova Scotia.

But that's not the first seemingly preposterous part of this true tale. First, there's Leonard's comically complex connection to his distant relative. This outstanding man was Leonard Gaudet's great, great, great, great, great, great, grandfather, three times over! Leonard told me he is directly descended from Jacques Maurice in three different ways. In other words, he had three great (x 6) grandfathers and they were all the same man! Got it?

I tried to keep the car on the road as Leonard laughingly explained. It was really very simple. You see, Jacques Maurice married his first wife in 1725. They had five sons. She died. Then Jacques Maurice married again to a woman who already had daughters from her first marriage. And so this group formed a family. That's the way they all became the

Acadian Brady Bunch. But in this case, well…imagine a semi-incestu-ous Brady Bunch. Sort of.

"Jacques' sons by his first wife," said Leonard, chuckling, "married his second wife's daughters!"

They married their stepsisters. So his stepdaughters also became his daughters-in-law. His sons' wives were also his sons' half-sisters. And their sons were both their own children and their own step-nephews! And those same children were Jacques Maurice's step-grandchildren and his grandchildren. No, I am not making this up. These marriages were real, though odd, parts of a rather gnarled Acadian family tree. It was more like a bush, really. A poorly pruned bush.

Besides the initial 'Brady-style' grouping, there were several other intertwinings and overlappings of the Vigneau-Gaudet family tree branches, down through generations. Apparently trees like these grow aplenty in Nova Scotia's family forest primeval.

Just ask genial genealogist Terry Punch, Nova Scotia's family tree expert. I checked with Terry a few days after depositing Leonard in Pictou town and driving off for my own mom's meal.

Terry assured me not only is such a pedigree possible in Nova Scotia, it's common in small Acadian populations. These conundrums of connections are all above board and completely within the Canon Law of the Roman Church, and within civil law too. So long as the mar-riages and remarriages were not between close blood relatives. Which they weren't. And yet, how curious and bizarre it is: Three separate family lines, from the one man, all leading down eight generations to my passenger pal Leonard. From hero to hitchhiker, both trying to get to home on a shoestring, some 240 years apart.

Shrewd and savvy, Jacques Maurice Vigneau was a businessman who grew up near the French fort at Port Royal. Later, the British took the fort and renamed it Annapolis Royal. The two solitudes were developing attitude. As a merchant with transport ships, Jacques Maurice skillfully navigated the increasingly stormy waters of French-English relations. In an age of ransoming captives, he made a business of exchanging prison-ers. He was a trusted neutral. Somehow he also managed to remain friends with the Mi'kmaq and the Huron peoples. He sailed a tight course. His diplomatic charm and talent for negotiation kept him and his large family and other Acadians alive during very tense times.

There is some evidence that his dealings were at times shady—extortion scams and prisoner ransoming for example. He had a dark reputation in some areas. But his powerful personal will, his commitment to his sense of home and his people, shines through the nightmare of the expulsion tragedy. He was the kind of man they needed.

I learned more about Jacques Maurice's heroic journey from Dr. Geoffrey Plank, a history professor at the University of Cincinnati, Ohio. He too hitched a ride on Leonard's family research, to write an academic paper called "Jacques Maurice Vigneau and the Meaning of Acadian Neutrality."

On a ship of almost a hundred Acadians, Jacques Maurice was expelled from his homeland, down to Georgia. But once there, he began immediately convincing British authorities to let his whole group leave. With no ship, they acquired about a dozen canoes. Keeping their travel plans secret, a hundred paddlers began creeping up the coastline to the next colony. Once on shore he talked his way into a safe release and they were on their way again. What's striking is that Jacques Maurice Vigneau repeated this several times. Dr. Plank was amazed at the gutsy voyage.

"In South Carolina, North Carolina, and New York, Vigneau charms the governor and convinces him, after initial hostility, to let him keep paddling his canoes up the Atlantic coast," he said.

"They go through Connecticut and Rhode Island," said Dr. Plank, "then reach Massachusetts which was always the most actively anti-Acadian of the colonies."

How did he manage to win passage from British authorities for his one hundred French Acadian friends? That's another peculiar piece of this true saga.

"He keeps calling them his family as they go up the coast," said Dr. Plank. The British bought the story. The canoes were allowed to pass. A single family seemed harmless. Even a big extended family, I guess. But eventually the paddlers found themselves up a creek.

Massachusetts authorities refused to let Jacques Maurice's flotilla proceed to Nova Scotia. They squeezed him for information.

"He finally admits," said Dr. Plank,"that only about one-fifth of these people are directly related to him. They might have been related some way, but I don't know."

Given his own family tree, maybe even Jacques Maurice himself didn't know if the hundred paddlers were all related to him. It could happen.

His luck had run dry. Their canoes were confiscated. They were forced to settle in Massachusetts. But this fellow never gave up. He actually petitioned to be paid for the value of the canoes; seven pounds, eight shillings and two pence. It was a nest egg to hatch a new scheme to get home. Always, home was in mind.

From destitution, Jacques Maurice rebuilt his shipping business in Massachusetts. Years passed. The Peace Treaty of 1763 allowed the Acadians to finally leave, though British-dominated Nova Scotia remained off limits. Typical of Jacques Maurice Vigneau's sharp deal making, he bargained as close as possible to his 'asking price' if you will.

He and his large family became founding settlers on the French-owned island of Miquelon, between Newfoundland and Nova Scotia. He was offered resettlement in the Caribbean but refused. He loved our Atlantic coast too much.

"I admire him," said Dr. Plank. "He really made the most of a horrible situation. The resiliency of him is absolutely amazing. It's very striking how resourceful he was. I'm also inspired by his devotion to his home and to his family. He did all of these things with a certain consistency; that he wanted to live in or at least near Nova Scotia."

Two and a half centuries later, Jacques Maurice Vigneau's descendent Leonard Gaudet doesn't paddle but hitchhikes 'home,' sharing the same sense of heartfelt belonging and rootedness here that motivated his distant family hero.

To end as we opened, here's a final fluke of fate. The strange hitchhikers' galaxy converged on itself a third time. After I had stopped my car for Leonard twice in two years, my own mother—she of the

Thanksgiving dinner—offered a lonely hitchhiker a ride near Pictou the following summer. It was Leonard! They got to talking and he learned of her connection to me, his usual driver who had listened to his whole story. He couldn't believe it. And he couldn't believe that she would stop for him. But she's like that. I guess I come by it naturally.

Shot Out of the Sky

A burning plane bail-out over hostile Germany.

L uck ran out on two Nova Scotians flying in a Halifax bomber through anti-aircraft blasts over Hanover, Germany in 1945. Both had over thirty successful bombing runs under their belts but this one would be different.

Doug Johnston of River Hebert, Cumberland County was the wireless operator on that ill-fated flight. John Dodge of Dartmouth was the navigator. Their plane, one of four hundred droning bombers in that Royal Canadian Air Force squadron, was attacked from underneath by a German fighter. "It caught fire immediately," said Doug.

Everyone had to bail out fast. "Our plane was blazing," he said. "One of the gas tanks exploded and we were in a steep dive."

Doug jumped out. "I went right up under the belly of the aircraft which was on fire," he told me matter-of-factly from his home in Willowdale, Ontario.

But John was first out of the escape hatch, with one big problem: he forgot where he was! "We were supposed to go out feet-first, facing aft," said John, chuckling. "Well, I dove out head first because I was used to swimming!"

"I came out in a terrific spin!," he said. Stretching out his arms, he pulled out of it, controlling his fall as best he could amid enemy gun blasts and aircraft air-streams that roughly buffeted the white, silk parachutes.

He didn't count on what happened next. Looking below, he thought he saw white clouds. "I figured I'd have another five thousand feet to go," said John, "but when I hit the clouds, I hit the ground!"

Turns out, the 'clouds' were just a white ground mist. He hit the earth hard and fast. And yet, landing in woods, he rolled properly and was unhurt.

Doug Johnston landed safely near a river. Both men hid their chutes, then hid themselves, in separate barns. The next day, both set out—separately—on foot, trying not to stand out in hostile German territory. Nevertheless, they both bumped into German soldiers, were captured, interrogated, and threatened. John was beaten by a group of Germans.

The two airmen were reunited in a German prison. "The worst," said John, "was the rats and dirt and they didn't give us any food. We spent a miserable time there."

Moved to another prisoner-of-war camp near Nuremburg, the two men endured the terrifying sounds of their own allied bombs falling nearby. "They were flying right over us," said Doug. "We could feel the tremors and shock waves in the huts. The chimneys would shake and sometimes come down."

Food was scarce. The Germans served a soup of boiled cabbage that men ate, knowing they'd be sick from it.

All prisoners were forcibly marched nine days in icy weather, with no food, towards Munich to another prison camp. During the march, allied airplanes approached. "We thought they were going to be friendly to us," said Doug, "They flew over, came back and strafed us! I dove into a ditch full of water. It was better than getting hit by our own bullets!"

John helped keep his marching comrades alive, using his salesman's skills to acquire food. "I didn't smoke," he said, "and I had some cigarettes from Red Cross parcels and I traded with natives along the route."

One day, while camped in an open field, the ragged prisoners wisely and quickly scrambled when an American Mustang flew over in attack mode. Using their bodies, they formed the letters P.O.W. on the ground and the pilot withheld his fire.

Once in the prison near Munich, the men endured until May 7, the same year. That morning, they woke up and the German guards were gone!

After a raging battle heard nearby, soon "cheering broke out among those nearest the main gate."

"We all made our way to see what was going on," said Doug, "and there were three American tanks there, three great big tanks; just a wonderful sight to see!"

"There was a tremendous celebration," said John.

Joyous prisoners clambered all over the friendly tanks. They were free!

Over half a century later, these two Nova Scotian airmen, Doug Johnston and John Dodge, are still friends, friends who will never forget what World War Two was all about.

Doug Johnston and John Dodge in better times, recalling their wartime near-death escape.

"You don't want to overlook that word freedom," said Doug, "freedom to worship and to travel and to talk like we are."

"We wouldn't have had that," he said, "if we hadn't fought this war and I think that's something that people should bear in mind: never take freedom for granted."

Lest we forget.

The Dutch Village Philosopher

Early ecologist hiked our heartland for science.

They called him the 'Dutch Village Philosopher.' Titus Smith was a studious, scientific thinker, yet rugged enough to explore all of mainland Nova Scotia's deep wooded interior, on foot! This natural history pioneer was one complex dude.

His three long woodsy treks between 1801 and 1802 boggle this weekend hiker's mind.

It was Lieutenant Governor Sir John Wentworth who sent Smith into Nova Scotia's heartland to "visit the most unfrequented parts, particularly the banks and borders of the different rivers, lakes and swamps and the richest uplands." Smith would collect data on the condition of soil and timber for the ship-building market.

But he went a bit overboard.

His first hike took him from Halifax up to the Musquodoboit area in Halifax County, on through the bush of Guysborough County, across Antigonish County, into Pictou County, then back down the middle of the province to Halifax. He hiked it in just six weeks.

David Hopper, a geographer and environmental planner in Halifax, wants to map these Titus treks. He is absolutely awed.

"I've walked some of the bush in Guysborough County and Halifax County and it is a tangle to get through," said Hopper when I met him at his downtown Natural Resources office, "Especially in the wetland areas."

Not to mention there was not even an ox cart track for most of it and "he went through all kinds of weather."

Amazing persistence!

"Keep in mind they (Smith and his assistant, a Mr.Carter) probably carried some pretty heavy stuff," said Hopper.

This unyielding naturalist later walked the other end of the province as well. Not along the beaches, but through the thick forests.

"All the way down the south shore, into Yarmouth, he circled back through Digby County, Annapolis, Kings and then circled back to Halifax," said Hopper. "It's a considerable distance."

To cover the northern end of the province Smith walked to the Minas Basin, took a boat across to Parrsboro, walked up and down the Cumberland County area, down past Truro and back to Halifax.

All before steroids!

He brought back meticulously hand-written journals, ink drawings of plants, floral lists and descriptions, and a hand-drawn map which remained the only general map of Nova Scotia for some thirty years afterwards. He detailed forests, rivers, geological features and wildlife. He commented on the moose, beaver, and the scarcity of caribou, now gone from the province altogether. He was a one-man natural history powerhouse on the move.

A granite tribute to a hardcore ecologist Titus Smith.

Titus Smith was the son of Loyalists. His father was a Yale graduate.

"A self-taught scientist, Smith was home schooled," said Hopper. "At the age of four he could read English books with ease, at seven he gained considerable proficiency in Latin. He also was learning Greek as well as studying German and French."

Despite his higher learning, he earned his income not as a scientist but as a simple land surveyor. He was also a farmer. In his vast gardens in the Dutch Village part of Halifax (now the Fairview area) he conducted plant and seed experiments. Some say his work was likely the first major contribution to plant ecology in North America. He learned agriculture, horticulture, and botany.

"There was very little he didn't know something about, and quite a lot that he knew a great deal about," says Terry Punch, a Halifax historian who trekked through Smith's life. "They used to call a person like that a polymath or a renaissance man. He was holistic in his approach to the world around him."

That was our 'Philosopher of Dutch Village!' According to Punch, that title first appeared in 1828, in Joseph Howe's newspaper, *The Nova Scotian*.

A social thinker, Smith opposed industrial progress that conflicted with nature. Call him part environmentalist, part pantheist.

"He saw God almost as identical with nature," said Punch. "A providential God who supplied his bounty here on earth—or nature supplies his bounty—and we're here as stewards to look after it and not to destroy but to utilize it and pass it down."

That was the Titus Smith philosophy.

"He was definitely ahead of his time," Punch declared.

Smith's learning and experimenting continued all his life, and he was consulted for advice on just about anything.

By 1850 he was dead and buried on Smith land, now a small park and playground on the corner of busy Titus Street and Vimy Avenue in Halifax's old Dutch Village area.

His gray granite grave marker still stands on the park's edge, opposite the hilltop monument that is also dedicated to Nova Scotia's remarkable Dutch Village Philosopher.

The Bluenose and The Babe

Our link to Babe Ruth's baseball beginnings.

Is it possible that one of the greatest all-time home run hitters in the history of baseball got his start from a Nova Scotian? Absolutely. The man who first introduced a young Babe Ruth to baseball, coached him and mentored him for 12 school years, and remained in Babe's words "the greatest man I have ever known" was from Lingan, Cape Breton Island! No kidding.

He was Martin Leo Boutilier—born in 1872 in Lingan, although two Cape Breton genealogists tell me he came from the Bras d'Or Boutiliers. When the Lingan mine closed, the Boutilier family moved to Boston. Dr. Colin Howell, author of *Northern Sandlots; A Social History of Maritime Baseball*, discovered that Martin took the religious name Brother Matthias when he joined the Xaverian Brothers Christian order in Baltimore, Maryland.

That's where a hyper, rowdy, restless, young George Herman Ruth was raising heck. His bartender father couldn't handle him so he was off to the St. Mary's Industrial School for "incorrigible" boys—reform school. There, The Babe and the Brother met and the lad's life was changed forever.

As a teacher at the school, Brother Matthias's effect on the Great Bambino is a matter of record. Just ask the Babe Ruth Museum in Baltimore, like I did. Consult any Babe Ruth book. Even the Hollywood movie *The Babe*, starring John Goodman, offers a portrayal of an Irish-sounding Brother Matthias—closest they could come to a Cape Breton accent I suppose.

Matthias grew up with the industrial Cape Breton baseball culture of long ago when teams of miners played against each other. Baseball was part of him. So he passed it on to his young, troubled students. He

introduced the unruly, baby-faced boy to the joy of bat meeting ball;
the thrill of the CRACK!

Author Robert Creamer, in his book *Babe: The Legend Comes to Life*,
quotes Babe Ruth saying of Brother Matthias, "I was born as a hitter the
day I ever saw him hit a baseball."

Babe Ruth's granddaughter Linda Ruth-Tossetti still gives public
talks and deals with Babe Ruth questions every day. She confirmed for
me by phone from her home in Connecticut that this charismatic Cape
Breton holy man was first to put a bat in Babe Ruth's hands in the St.
Mary's schoolyard in 1902. It started with Babe heckling his classmates.

"Sitting on the wall one day
watching them play baseball, he
started teasing them," said Ruth-
Tossetti.

"Brother Matthias said 'if you
think you can do better, come up
and show us.'"

He did, and the rowdy Ruth
took a liking to the game. It gave
him a focus that changed his
ways. "He said in later years that
that actually saved his life," said
Ruth-Tossetti. "It kept him from
getting into a life of crime or
being dead!"

And it all started with that first
time at bat when young Ruth
belted the ball through a school
window and hit the school bell!

Brother Matthias, the first to put a bat
in Babe Ruth's hands.

The Xaverian Brothers later reversed the lay of the ball field, so the
young Bambino didn't smash any more glass.

Tall, tough and caring, Brother Matthias became Babe's mentor and
advisor from that day on, until his death. "Brother Matthias was very
imposing and very big. Babe respected him. He took time with Babe,"
said Ruth-Tossetti.

It was time well spent.

When Babe was still a teenager, he was drafted into pro ball straight from Matthias's school team. Throughout his famous career, Ruth never ceased his wild, carousing ways. But Matthias's spirit tamed that in him just enough.

At the height of his fame, the rebellious Ruth, once headed for jail, became instead gregariously generous. Whether it was free hotdogs, autographs, or handfuls of money, the home-run king loved to give to young fans, especially sick children, just as Matthias had reached out to him. Ruth would sign autographs for little fans at Yankee Stadium until it grew dark.

He showed the same spirit when he came to Nova Scotia. His adopted daughter Julia Ruth Stevens, who was 79 when I reached her at her home in Arizona, was with him on that visit. She remembered that The Babe took time from his fishing trip for a surprise visit to children in hospital.

He came to eastern Canada often: fishing, golfing, hunting and doing special crowd-pleasing baseball appearances. He hit out a ball or two in Westville, Nova Scotia in 1936 and a few in Halifax in 1942.

When Brother Matthias died and was buried in Massachusetts in 1944, The Babe was too sick to attend his friend's funeral. He sent a young fan—a boy named Frankie—in his stead. The Babe died of cancer four years later.

All their lives, these two great men shared a special bond of baseball. It was a Nova Scotian connection Babe Ruth couldn't have lived without.

That's Amor, Eh?

An oddball Nova Scotian brings B.C. into the Canadian fold.

L et's face it, eccentric politicians—perhaps the best kind of politician—helped to build this country. We've had our fair share of them in this province. In fact, sometimes we even export them. One such country builder left Nova Scotia and travelled to that other sea-bound coast and brought British Columbia into the Canadian Confederation.

A man with a brilliant mind, he was born in Windsor, Nova Scotia, in 1825 but his infamous reputation was earned in B.C. Fascinating, eccentric, and versatile, he is best remembered for his unusual name: Bill Smith. Actually, I guess it was his name change that stood out. After leaving Nova Scotia, he dropped the plain and simple 'Bill Smith' and began calling himself by the flamboyant name 'Amor De Cosmos,' meaning lover of the universe.

I know what you're thinking. We sure know how to grow the peculiar politicos on this coast don't we? And you thought Howard Dill's giant pumpkins were Windsor's strangest crop! Well, Amor De Cosmos was a fast-growing politician who also got very big and colourful.

He was, a very bright Windsor lad. William (Bill) Alexander Smith attended King's College in that town. Later, at Dalhousie University in Halifax, he was on the debating club. Young Bill—I mean Amor—was a slightly spooky, entertaining, and smart fella.

Dr. Robert MacDonald, a University of British Columbia scholar with family ties to Pictou County, has studied this western politician. "He was a bit of a loner," said Dr. MacDonald on the long distance line. "He never married. He was very passionate, quite articulate, very well educated. His life was a very public life."

Amor's looks were also attention grabbing. "He wore a frock coat, top hat; a big-handled stick, which he wore as a pretentious prop, hung from his forearm."

This far into the description, Amor sounded affected but more or less harmless, and definitely talented—perhaps a nineteenth century Dennis Rodman? But then Dr. MacDonald described Amor's character. "He was quite egotistical. He had a habit of talking to people in a very lofty and superior manner."

Amor donned his pretentious new name while in the United States. He had left his home province to cross the American landscape on a rough wagon caravan ride fraught with raids by Natives. He landed amid the great California gold boom.

Like a naive tourist, he brought his camera and became one of the first to make good money at early photography.

He applied to have a private member's bill entered into the California legislature to change his name from plain Bill Smith to Amor De Cosmos. It's a combination of French, Latin, and Greek. Legislators jeered but Bill's bill passed. Asked why he chose it, Amor explained the name symbolized the things he loved most, namely "love of order, beauty, the world, and the universe." That's Amor, eh!

Nova Scotia's "Lover of the Universe" who brought British Columbia into Canada.

Perhaps Amor started California's reputation as the cosmic oddball capital of the world. Far out! Later, Amor De Cosmos moved north to Canada's lotus land. Far up! Up to the land that would become the province of British California…er, Columbia.

He left his birth name behind, but brought with him his Nova Scotian spirit. Amor became the Joe Howe of the west coast; like the great Nova Scotian defender of political freedoms, Amor also started a newspaper in which he openly and fearlessly criticized the colonial administration. He fought for responsible government. A true Howe-ist!

Like Howe, Amor jumped from the fifth estate to the political arena. In 1860, this lover of the universe ran for election for the first time. He ran often, winning and losing. At one election, his long, lavish name was called into question. He was forced to run as "William Alexander Smith, commonly known as Amor De Cosmos." It made for a lengthy ballot.

That was before the days of Grits versus Tories. Amor was a sort of pre-Liberal Liberal. "He was a 'small L' liberal," said Dr. MacDonald. "He believed in the rights of ordinary people, in representative government."

However, Amor was not a democrat. "He would believe that voters should own some property to gain full democratic rights."

As Howe did, B.C. politicians came to appreciate Confederation as a good thing, joining in 1871. Amor became a member for Victoria District, provincial premier, and one of the first elected B.C. federal M.P.s, all at once! An early double—or triple—dipper.

During his short premiership, this cosmic romantic brought in responsible government, including the secret ballot for B.C. voters. Joe Howe would have been proud.

And yet, the universe wasn't unfolding as it should have for Amor. In 1882, the oddly-named politician was defeated by—I kid you not—Noah Shakespeare. But what's in a name? Certainly the B.C. voters were amused if not well-led.

Amor's name, appearance, and personality might have been unusual, but his political skills were highly regarded. Nevertheless, he was eventually ousted for good.

He spent his remaining years wandering the streets neglected, still with his fancy frock and pretentious cane. He drank, got into fistfights, was declared of unsound mind, and died at age 70 in 1897.

Lonely, drunk, and insane after a life in B.C. politics? I can see that.

Amor was a long way from his boyhood days in tranquil Windsor, Nova Scotia. A universe away. But his star shone brightly in those crucial years of Canada's genesis.

On Top
of the Great Explosion

A lucky firefighter survives when
a munitions ship explodes before his eyes.

In early December 1917, a single injured fireman lay in his hospital bed, no doubt amazed at his miraculous survival. Halifax and Dartmouth were in shock. In the aftermath of the harbour explosion, hundreds of people lay dead, the injured suffered, children cried for lost parents, a city staggered.

The fireman was Billy Wells. He was among the crew of the *Patricia*, the Halifax firetruck that responded to what was at first just a ship fire at Pier 6, that December 6th morning. Long, sleek, and shiny, the *Patricia* was the first piece of motorized fire apparatus in Canada.

The rest of her crew were: Captain William Broderick, Walter Hennessey, Frank Killeen, Frank Leahy, and Captain Michael Maltus. Maltus had replaced a man who had the flu, a sick bug that, in a twist of fate, saved the ill man's life.

John Duggan responded to the fire from another station on the horse-drawn #4 hose-wagon. Firechief Condon and his deputy, a man named Brunt, responded in the Chief's beautiful brand-new MacLaughlin Buick roadster.

Another fireman, named Albert Brunt, met the *Patricia* speeding to the fire, tried to jump on the back runningboard and missed, skinning his knees badly. The men on back of the *Patricia* waved and hooted at him, laughing on their route to death.

These details come from Dave Singer, a modern-day fire engine driver in Halifax who diligently researched these men's final minutes on the explosion day.

"Feeling the great heat from where the *Mont Blanc* had brushed up against Pier 6, the Chief began giving orders," said Singer.

"He told Capt. Broderick to have them run all the hose they had from the *Patricia* out to the ship and they would wait for the other gear to arrive," he said.

The other gear never had a chance to arrive.

Billy Wells was at the wheel of the *Patsy*, backing up to the fire hydrant at the foot of Richmond Street, just across the road from the burning munitions ship, *Mont Blanc*. The vessel was loaded with wartime explosives and lighted like a giant sick of dynamite.

A few minutes past 9:00 A.M....it blew. A massive, deafening explosion blasted high and wide, destroying the north end of Halifax—a blast so enormous it was heard in Prince Edward Island.

The immense burst of power blew deep scars into the harbour floor, threw tonnes of metal across the city and shattered buildings all around.

And those Halifax firefighters were working at ground zero, right on top of the blast. All were killed, except one: the driver, Billy Wells.

"He was in quite a state," said Singer. "All the muscles were torn from his right arm, his right eye was hanging out on this cheek and all he had left on was his pants and one boot."

But it wasn't over. "He was bleeding quite profusely when the tidal wave

Halifax explosion damage: one fireman walked away from the core of the blast.

came up from the harbour, driving him up Richmond Hill," said Singer.

"He came back down with the tidal wave, got caught up in the telegraph wires and was still conscious."

Dazed and losing consciousness, he looked up to see the unconsumed gun cotton from the munitions ship falling from the sky like a black rain; a sooty, charred mess.

Wells was coated.

"He was quite black and bloody." But still alive.

Devastation stretched around him. He saw the wrecked *Patricia* and looked down to see her broken steering wheel still tightly gripped in his hand. His jolt from the vehicle was so rapid his brain didn't have the split second required to tell his fingers to let go.

He staggered forward, still doing his duty. "He came across two children crying in the street," said Singer. He

handed them on to two sailors, passed the chief's destroyed car, then "went on, fell down and passed out again."

He was picked up and taken to the chaos of a hospital trying to cope with all the victims. He lay, bleeding and weak, for two days in a hallway until he could be treated.

Permanently scarred, he lived and worked his whole life in Halifax, his last years as a jovial crossing guard at Russell and Gottingen streets, near the

The wrecked *Patricia* in front of the Brunswick Street fire station.

explosion site. He died in 1971.

The *Patricia*'s steering wheel that survived the explosion with him is kept at the Lady Hammond Road fire station in north end Halifax where a monument also stands as a memorial to these firemen who lost their lives serving their city.

In 1992, on the day Dave Singer saw the memorial he helped erect unveiled, he walked through the snow of two city cemeteries in his smart blue Halifax Fire Department uniform. He was visiting the gravesites of his fellow firemen, killed in the line of duty back in 1917. At each gravestone that he had traced through his off duty research, he placed a wreath. It was his personal salute to his fallen comrades of the fire service in his home city.

He's been going grave to grave replacing those wreaths every December 6th since, remembering.

Congressional Medal Brothers

Local heroes risked their lives attacking Cuba.

Two Nova Scotians were the first brothers to be awarded together the prestigious American Congressional Medal of Honor for bravery in battle. Willard and Harry Miller of Noel Shore, Hants County pulled off an impossible mission under heavy gunfire in a Cuban bay a century ago.

Their birth house in Noel Shore bears a brass plaque referring to the "brother heroes" who "in 1898 were crew members of the American gunboat *Nashville* serving in the Spanish-American war." The Miller boys "took part in a daring and dangerous action."

Born to a master shipbuilder in the late 1870s, Harry and Willard left home as rebellious teens, winding up in Massachusetts.

Surprisingly, this history comes from Harry's own son. Born when Harry was sixty years old, Bill Miller is now near that age himself and remembers listening to his father's navy stories of things that happened in the 1890s!

Quite a leap back in time, from one memory handed down to the next.

Born in Costa Rica, Bill talked to me over the phone in broken English, spiced with a Spanish accent. He said his father and uncle

Willard enlisted in the American Navy for the thrill.

"My father say he don't care; he just want to go away and see the world. Just like an adventure," he said.

The American Navy was engaging the Spanish in war at Cienfuegos, Cuba. The Miller brothers were among the crew of U.S.S. *Nashville* who volunteered to set out in small boats to cut the two underwater transatlantic communication cables between Spain and Cuba.

Simple sabotage. Cutting the communication lines was crucial to winning the war. The cables were reachable only where they came on shore in Cuba. "They had to go close to the coast," said Bill, "where the enemy batteries were and all these Spanish soldiers."

The two Miller brothers sailed in separate boats with about eight crew members in each. They were told it was a suicide mission. The night before the raid, the sailors wrote their wills and farewell letters to their loved ones.

The next day, the little boats, at risk of smashing on coastal rocks, moved in with *Nashville* shooting protective cover shots at the Spanish on shore. The men saw the cables through the water and snagged them with a long gaff hook while their own ship's shells zipped dangerously close over their heads. The return enemy fire rained down.

In the winter of 1900, Harry Miller wrote about his mission impossible for the *Noel Shore Journal*: "The bullets began whizzing about our heads like a swarm of hornets."

One man was shot through the head, his jaw torn away.

The Miller brothers helped with the two cables as the blacksmith sawed them with a large hack saw. They worked feverishly as cannons blasted the nearby shore.

"The people on land was shooting on the ship too," said Bill, "With all the smoke and everything they say they were just lucky to survive it. But they cut the cable!"

Mission accomplished!

But heavy crossfire continued. Harry Miller fired on a Spanish gunman in the top of the lighthouse—that stopped some enemy gunfire. But Harry's officer had three fingers shot off. And Harry felt a hot bullet whiz by his face with a buzz like a mosquito. The man behind him groaned and fell dead on Harry's back.

"He said that he'd never forget the fellow that was by his side," said Bill. "But nothing happened to my father; not a scratch."

Luck lives between the bullets. Harry and Willard survived. Their boats returned to U.S.S. *Nashville* where three more dead crewmen were lowered into a watery grave. Some reports said over three hundred Spaniards were killed in that battle.

Two Nova Scotian men on U.S.S. *Nashville* helped attack Cuba.

A year later, the brothers Miller received their Congressional Medals, each a five-point star, for courage displayed under enemy fire.

Willard Miller died in 1959 and is buried as an American navy hero in grave #46-15 of Arlington National Cemetery. Harry Miller passed away at age 89, in 1968. He is buried in Costa Rica where he had settled after his navy service to work building rail bridges. His chosen wife—here's irony—was of Spanish heritage. Hence Bill's accent.

But I didn't call Bill Miller down in those hot Costa Rican climes. Believe it or not, in 1974, over three-quarters of a century after his father left here, Bill moved back to the land of his father's roots—Hants County, Nova Scotia. He works on a farm in Poplar Grove, near Windsor.

His father's medal is with relatives in Costa Rica. His father's legacy—and his uncle's—is proudly preserved in Miller family memory.

(Thanks again to champion story contributor "Agnes Miller of Kentville, Nova Scotia" whose letter alerting me to these brothers' brass plaque on the Noel Shore is part of the cover design of this book's predecessor, *History with a Twist*, 1998.)

Babes in the Wood

An ancient story motif takes on a tragic realism in Nova Scotia.

A mere "babe in the wood"—that's what some call the naive or inexperienced. This very old English expression is intricately linked with a heart-wrenching incident on the edge of Dartmouth, in woods near Preston, in the mid-1800s.

The tragedy of that Dartmouth event is documented in an old song written by Daniel Blois. Nova Scotian song collector Helen Creighton's recording of that tune is preserved at our friendly provincial archives:

In 1800 and 42,
April the eleventh day
Two little girls from Preston Road into the woods did stray…

This true story is every parent's nightmare: Mere babes lost in woods.

The song—sometimes called "Meagher's Children" or "Babes in the Wood"—describes the two lost little sisters of the Meagher family: Jane Elizabeth, age six, and Margaret, age four.

The Meaghers lived near the old Preston Road, now Highway #7, in the Westphal area of Dartmouth, near Loon Lake. In 1842, the two little girls just wandered away from home.

I asked Anita Price, curator of the Dartmouth Heritage Museum, to reread some newsprint accounts and describe what happened. "They went off into the woods berry picking or looking for spruce gum or foraging and they got lost," she said.

The Meaghers were a couple with four children. At the time, the mother was confined to her room with an infant and the father was down with a case of measles. But by the end of the day he was up from his sickbed, summoning the neighbours, scouring the woods, yelling his young daughters' names. They searched all that night by lighted torch with no luck.

Dartmouth's historical writer the late Dr. John Martin referenced newspapers of the day. According to him, searchers arrived at the home of a Black family. The son had thought he heard something but his parents dismissed it as animal noises. Some accounts, the song included, wrongly accused that family of not caring.

In fact, it seems everyone cared.

"Soldiers from the forts, sailors from the wharfs, people from the Mi'kmaq community, from Preston—the Black community—all showed up and were helping to look for these kids." said Price.

"It was a real community effort," she said.

Folklore meets fact at grave of two little girls in Dartmouth.

But the woods were dense. April's weather grew cold. Two inches of snow fell the second day. Yet, the whole area was wild with activity. People poured across the harbour from Halifax to help search, others stood at the ferry gates awaiting news.

Later they learned that the lost little girls not only faced the cold in skimpy clothing and cracked shoes but they had suffered injuries.

"The older girl was badly cut and had used her clothing to try to tie a bandage around her leg and feet because they were travelling some distance through that sort of terrain," she said. "They really weren't ready for it."

And who could be ready for what searchers finally found after a week-long search? Two little cold bodies, curled together.

"The youngest child was wrapped in the older child's arms, and the older child had tried to put her clothing over her little sister to keep her warm," said Price.

"Considering the ages, it was incredible nurturing that they kept care of each other like that," she said.

A sorrowful tragedy. But it was also a case of life imitating art.

The motif of children lost in woods is actually centuries old. An old Victorian children's book out of England called *Babes in the Wood*, illustrated by R. Caldecott, describes the tale of an evil uncle who, wanting to collect an inheritance, leaves two young siblings to wander and die in woods. Perhaps you remember the book from your childhood? The circumstances of those storybook deaths are similar to the Meagher children's sad demise.

That old song about the 1842 event also mixes reality with folk fiction. Phillip Hiscock, a folklore researcher at Memorial University in Newfoundland, believes the Nova Scotian songwriter Blois was aware of another older, similar folk tune as he wrote about the tragedy in Dartmouth woods.

"He probably said to himself 'that's just like that old song, 'Babes in the Wood,' which was at least 150 years older than he was," said Hiscock by phone to me from Newfoundland.

The repeated story of lost babes in woods is older still.

"There are traces going back to the end of the 1500s, probably to an actual event," he said.

Borrowed from that long legacy of lore, the expression "babes in the wood" was inscribed into the large metal plaque at the Meagher children's gravesite at Dartmouth's Woodlawn Cemetery.

It is said the two little sisters lie in one coffin, with arms around each other, as they were found in the woods, just as the children in the old Caldecott storybook lay in death together, like fact with folklore, intertwined forever.

A Movie Munchkin in our Midst!

A small Bluenose-born actor makes it big in the land of Oz!

"Toto, I've a feeling we're not in Kansas anymore."

You're not in Nova Scotia either Dorothy but there's a Bluenose-born Munchkin standing right beside you! That's right, one of the taller—if not the tallest—of the many Munchkins of Munchkinland in the classic 1939 film *The Wizard of Oz* was from this province. It's no tall tale. He was Murray Wood, a diminutive actor, singer and dancer, born here on June 12, 1908.

I was tipped to this tiny actor when entertainment writer Ian Johnston pleaded in his *Daily News* column for information from his readers on this link to the land of Oz. He had a brief obituary from the United States. Murray passed away, age 91, in September of 1999. There was a mere mention of this Munchkin's Bluenose roots. Ian wanted more. Me too.

Many calls later, via *Classic Images Magazine* in Arizona and the *Miami Herald* newspaper, I found the widow of this Munchkin. Jean Wood is 84 and lives in Miami, Florida. Reached by phone, she confirmed that whenever her late husband was asked where he came from, he always said "Nova Scotia." His family had a farm in the Prospect area, near Halifax.

Believed to be the tallest of over a hundred little people in the Oz movie, Murray Wood was four feet two inches. Jean told me you can see him in the famous scene in which the Mayor of Munchkinland greets Dorothy (Judy Garland). "He is standing next to the left arm of Judy Garland," said Jean. Murray wore "a long blue robe with a turned up collar." It has flower crests on each shoulder. That's our Munchkin!

He also plays a front row soldier in the Munchkin parade scene.

He came from a Nova Scotian family of seven children—all of average height except him. A brother was six feet two inches.

The Wood family moved to Leominister, Massachusetts when Murray was about five or eight. The parents later split. Father Charles E. Wood returned and is buried in Nova Scotia, possibly Halifax.

Murray's mother, Julia Elizabeth Wood, once a nurse at a Halifax hospital, raised the children.

Murray learned to tap dance and sing. At about 17, he went to New York and was discovered. Standing on the corner of Broadway, "an agent walked up and asked if he sang or danced," said Jean. He began playing the theatres there. Later he performed at the Roxy Nightclub, Radio City Music Hall with Kate Smith, up and down the Californian coast, and he even shared a stage with Jackie Gleason.

Murray always claimed he helped two other big

Nova Scotian Munchkin Murray Wood in long robe at back, between Dorothy and the Mayor of Munchkinland.

acts get started. Standing outside a New York theatre having a smoke one day, three girls approached him. They sang for Murray, he introduced them to orchestra leader Larry Rich and the rest was entertainment history. They were the Andrews Sisters. Murray apparently gave the same kind of break to a young, new comedian—Red Skelton.

Jean and Murray were a nightclub duo. A singer, Jean was just a few inches taller than he, at four feet six. They fell for each other while working a casino in Philadelphia and married in 1948.

Jean cheerfully described how, as a stage couple married for 52 years, they were a real team. They performed together for over thirty years in Miami and along the eastern seaboard. They worked ninety hotels in four months, doing two and three shows a night at times! She and Murray were small but they had big voices. "Murray was a wonderful master of ceremonies," Jean exclaimed.

"Murray and I would sing and we had all special arrangements made up. We would open with a number called 'Sitting on a Doorstep' which Murray wrote. We'd do mostly Cole Porter tunes. We'd do cute little gags and things together," she said.

In an episode of the TV series "Gentle Ben," Murray played a carnival character. But *The Wizard of Oz* was his only movie credit. He and Jean rode the wave of the Wizard of Oz popularity for years, often performing Judy Garland's well-known solo. "He used to sing the song 'Over the Rainbow' in the nightclubs," said Jean. "He would sing singly and then I would sing singly and then we'd sing together."

At that point in our long distance phone chat Jean giddily succumbed to my request and she sang. In her old stage voice—fragile but still clear and precise—Jean sang just the first lyric line from that classic tune that touched generations of movie lovers. "Some wherrre…oooover the rainnnnbow…way up highhhhh…"

It was a magic moment reminiscent of a great event in grand old American show business—*The Wizard of Oz*. And Nova Scotia's own Munchkin, Murray Wood, was part of it.

Anna and the King on a Halifax Pier

How the famous King of Siam governess ended up on our shores.

There must be something special about the story of Anna and the King. It's been a big screen Hollywood feature starring the famous Jodie Foster. It's been a 1951 Rodgers and Hammerstein musical. It's been published and lectured on academically. It has even charmed the children as an animated TV series. Anna has been biographied to death since her death. So, who was this celebrated Anna, really? Why is there a Halifax art gallery named after her? Here's why: She was one heck of a fascinating, complex woman who served the King of Siam before adopting Victorian Halifax as her home for almost twenty years.

Some facts of Anna Leonowens' life have been fudged or fuzzified, even by her. To help set things straight, I tracked down ancestral and archival sources. Lois Yorke of the Nova Scotia Archives recently discovered a stash of Anna's personal letters in another archive near Chicago.

Here's what I learned from Lois: Anna Leonowens was governess to the 67 children of King Mongkut of Siam in the 1860s. That's right, 67. She was born in 1831 of European and perhaps East Indian ancestry. Raised as an army brat in various British army stations in India, she had an uneasy upbringing. Her name was Ann Harriet Emma Edwards, but she adopted the name Anna. She married Thomas Leon Owens. By the time he died, she had adopted and combined his names as her last name: Leonowens. It's not clear why she did that.

Perhaps it was to sharpen her image, to help sell her books, to support her family. Widowed young, Anna was a writer and teacher. Those skills got her into Siam where she had some influence on King Mongkut during very tense political times. Siam—now Thailand—was fighting off imperialist aggressions from France and Britain. As a personal secretary and liaison, Anna the governess helped the king write letters of state.

"In shaping the letters and choosing the words, she certainly was having an influence on the development of diplomatics in South East Asia," said Ms. Yorke.

Cool! O.K., so how did this influential Anna end up here in Bluenose country? After five years in Siam, she lived in New York, joined the posh literary scene, and published books about her Siamese years. None of them mentions a love affair with the king, or with Yul Brynner for that matter.

That's just Hollywood.

Her great granddaughter, 84-year-old Ann Fairlie of Toronto,

Anna Leonowens pushed for tax revolt in Nova Scotia.

was happy to tell me more about her famous ancestor when I reached her by phone. She told me Anna Leonowens moved to Halifax from New York because "her daughter married Thomas Fyshe who was made the general manager of the Bank of Nova Scotia. She came with them to Halifax and threw her weight around there."

Anna certainly caught our little port city off-guard. Halifax of the 1880s and 90s was a little restrictive for this brilliant, compassionate, irrepressible, well-travelled woman. So she started agitating. Author Leslie Smith Dow, in her book *Anna Leonowens; A Life Beyond the King and I*, says Anna encouraged a tax revolt by Nova Scotian women denied the right to vote—a pre-feminism feminist! Always encouraging culture appreciation, Anna fought to found an early art school which became the Nova Scotia College of Art and Design. (Hey, thanks Anna! I enjoyed my year at NSCAD.)

Good learning was high on her list. Despite her efforts to bring a bit more polish to this military port city, Anna saw that her grandchildren studied abroad.

"My father (Thomas Fyshe) was brought up, pretty well, by Anna," said Mrs. Fairlie, who used to be Ann Fyshe. "They knew her as rather stern, very keen on education. She took four of them to Germany for educating."

Anna, her daughter Avis Fyshe, and Avis' children stayed in Germany almost five years. The bank manager husband stayed in Halifax, alone.

In 1897, Anna said farewell to Nova Scotia. She resettled in Montreal where she died in 1915. Hers was an amazing life that left an indelible mark on our capital city.

A Nazi in Paradise

Hitler's henchman issued party propaganda from the Annapolis Valley.

I am still amazed, as I continue digging into the stories of this sea-bound place, at the many ways this magical province inserts itself into so many major events in world history. Surely no other piece of the planet touches the highlights of history's time line like this one. This is no hyperbole. There's just something special about Nova Scotia's past. Here, for example, I find myself writing of a Nazi in Paradise! That's Paradise, Nova Scotia by the way, in our Annapolis Valley. Yes, Adolph Hitler's close aide—a founding member of the Nazi Party—lived here among us during the war.

His name was Otto Strasser. He and his brother Gregor were members of Hitler's fledgling National-Socialist party in the early 1920s. A highly intelligent activist, Strasser was a German newspaper publisher courted by Hitler. As a journalist, Strasser had interviewed Hitler many times in the years leading up to the fanatical leader's rise to power.

Strasser wrote about the Nazi cause.

Most written accounts, including his own book called *Hitler and I*, describe Otto Strasser and his brother as fervent German patriots. Both contributed to Hitler's National Socialist party in its earliest stages, post-World War One.

Hitler sent Otto's brother Gregor Strasser to organize the north of the country, along with the infamous Mr. Goebbels. But Otto continued publishing articles pushing for a new direction for the Nazi party, more to the left.

Nazi Otto Strasser lived among our apple blossoms.

Heated verbal fights were waged between Hitler and Otto Strasser. The inevitable schism erupted in 1930. It was the first major ideological split from Hitler's movement.

Brother Gregor remained in Hitler's party but was killed for showing dissent. Otto, afraid for his life, skipped town, lived around Europe during the 1930s, then landed in Montreal. His stay in Quebec was brief. A Czechoslovakian friend in Nova Scotia invited Otto to move here. The breakaway Nazi arrived in the Annapolis Valley in 1941.

His first home in the province was Bridgetown. His landlady apparently complained he was an incompatible tenant. This exiled German then rented a small apartment above a Co-op store in Paradise, Annapolis County.

Now, *there's* a contradiction. Nazism and the Co-op movement!

Some villagers remember Otto Strasser. The Paradisians I talked with told me he was a very charming, polite, intelligent gentleman. The ladies loved him. He enjoyed chats with local schoolchildren. He apparently was friendly with another intellectual, former Premier Henry Hicks.

Much of this I learned from Paradise resident Allan Bishop, a bus driver. Allan's father rented the small apartment to Otto, his little piece of Paradise.

"I think people who really knew him," said Allan, "found him really friendly and they liked him very much."

But having a Nazi in their midst made a few folks nervous. Especially the ones who didn't really know him.

"Because he had been in the area during the war," said Allan, "I think they thought, 'well, he's got a radio here and he's in contact with Germany.'

"A lot of people certainly resented him being here."

Otto wasn't alone above the Co-op store. One resident told me he had a "secretary" with him. But Allan Bishop knows better. "He had a mistress, Margarita, originally from Germany," said Allan, "and she had gone out with him for a number of years."

Nazi love in Paradise? This story is a headline writer's dream. But Allan told me he wasn't sure what the whole story was. Otto apparently had a wife and children back in Germany whom he hadn't seen for about 16 years.

This Nazi in Nova Scotia didn't have a job. Maybe he was trying to blend in. I couldn't really see him bagging groceries at the Co-op anyway. He was supported by his other brother, who was also a Brother, a Benedictine monk in the United States. So just to update you, Otto was a dissident Nazi supported by a monk, living in sin in Paradise. Got it? No, I am not making this up.

He kept busy writing books and articles. They were sent overseas to promote his view of Nazism. Otto was trying to lead his political party, The League for Germany's Revival, from his four-room apartment in the Annapolis Valley.

His political views were quite different from Hitler's, or so he claimed. This exiled German in Nova Scotia was trying to rejuvenate Germany with his brand of national socialism, a brand he said was democratic. Otto wrote that he opposed Hitler's cozying up with capitalists and industrialists.

Professor Glen Wilkinson at Acadia University told me Otto Strasser's movement claimed to be true socialism but was in fact closer to Marxism. (Still a far cry from rural Co-operativism!) Otto's movement to advance his German party was known as the Black Front. Black referred to the dark, cloaked, secretive nature of the movement. He tried to keep it alive through the mail from the tiny post office in Paradise.

His book makes it clear that Otto envisioned the Black Front as a secret left wing of the Nazi party. But historians say it was not as powerful and popular as Otto's writings claim. And the Allies were skeptical of his intentions.

Fifty years ago the *Chronicle Herald* in Halifax reported on Otto Strasser's plight and pronouncements from the Annapolis Valley. When his book *Hitler and I* was banned from Germany by U.S. authorities in 1949, he raged that it was the "strangest move in the political witch hunt against me." He stated that the occupation authorities in Germany had approved his book prior to publication. He declared that his writings would go a long way to "opening the eyes of uncounted Frenchmen, Britishers, and Americans against the danger of Hitler and Hitlerism."

His voice was being heard but ignored. He was a prisoner of Paradise. Five times the Canadian government refused Otto Strasser a passport to return to his homeland. Further newspaper reports show that American military leaders were aware of Otto's split from Adolph but they still thought him a dangerous German influence. They weren't buying his pleas.

Same thing happened to Leon Trotsky during his 1917 imprisonment in Amherst (See my first book, *History with a Twist*). Plucked from a ship in Halifax Harbour, Trosky was detained in an Amherst prisoner of war camp until Canadian authorities could no longer justify keeping him. He left there immediately to join in fanning the fires of the Russian revolution and fueling the rise of communism.

I can't help but wonder what effect Otto might have had if allowed back to Germany at the right time. The ideological clash might have diluted Hitler's power before it peaked in the 1930s and a world war might have been diverted. Maybe.

Or, as the Allied leaders supposed, would Otto have become another kind of Hitler. Who knows? Otto was trapped here, in Nova Scotia.

It fascinates, really. One of the founders of the Nazi party, ensconced among our apple blossoms. Just another intertwining twist betwixt Nova Scotia and the world.

After the war, Otto Strasser was released to return to his German homeland in the mid-1950s. He lived his remaining years there, fearing for his life, surrounded by guards. His hopes of one day leading Germany had long faded.

Allan Bishop's mother visited Otto in his home country. She was welcomed and treated well.

Here comes the kicker.

According to Allan, Otto actually returned to Nova Scotia in postwar years on a new business venture. Apparently Nova Scotia's favorite seafood had made an impression on him. "He wrote my father," said Allan. "And he came back here with a bunch of German businessmen. He was promoting lobsters! That wasn't a big market at the time and he saw big possibilities!"

Let's get this straight now: Otto was a former Nazi/socialist, anti-Hitler, Paradise-escapee and pioneer lobster seller? Yup. It's true. It actually happened, right here. I'm telling you, there's something about this place.

Yeah, there's something about this place.

University of the Air

An early radio experiment fostered rural learning and...me!

May I speak personally for a moment? This story about early radio in Nova Scotia is a piece of my past. It touches close to home but it's also an interesting and documented part of Nova Scotia history, a part I know many in the northeastern end of the province will remember and appreciate. I am sure of that because I grew up meeting countless older folk who, upon hearing my surname, would always come out with "Well, I remember your father…" The inevitable memorable anecdote they'd been carrying about for years would come next. "I remember the time he was…" So, why so many memories held so dear by complete strangers? I had to do research to understand that because this all happened before my time. It hinges on a bold new venture in broadcasting in Nova Scotia. Let me take you back to March 25, 1943.

CJFX Radio in Antigonish signed on the air that day as an experiment in educational radio that grew from the internationally famous "Antigonish Movement," led by the legendary priest-professors Dr. Moses M. Coady and Fr. Jimmy Tompkins.

Saint Francis Xavier University's Extension Department was looking for new ways to reach out, to educate the farmers, fishermen, miners, and lumbermen in that end of the province. The Catholic University also hoped to counter other religious broadcasts with their own church's message. They gathered a group to look at their options. Among those invited was a friend of the university with radio experience at CJCB in Sydney—J. Clyde Nunn. Growing up in Whitney Pier, Cape Breton, he had tinkered with early radio sets as a boy. As a St.F.X.U. student he was part of the early founding of the Antigonish Movement, well immersed in the university's philosophy of outreach, of teaching people to become 'masters of their own destiny.' He suggested at that meeting the university start its own radio station.

He cautioned the group that of course such a venture would be impossible while there was still a war going on. The fiery activist Fr. Jimmy Tompkins had only to hear "impossible" to make him want to do it! So they looked into it. Nunn was commissioned by his alma mater to make it work. First there was the politics of getting a broadcast licence for this unusual concept during wartime. So, when Nunn went to Ottawa by train to argue for the licence, the powerful orator Dr. Moses Coady went with him for backup. They also had Senator Alex Johnston supporting them, the same politician who helped Marconi himself get his Cape Breton radio licence years earlier.

Needless to say, they got the licence.

Their letter of application in 1940 laid out their goal: "The proposed station would have for its chief objective the offering of programmes of broadly educational character which would be directed towards making the people it would serve better citizens and more appreciative of the spiritual, social and economic advantages of our democratic way of life."

Lofty sentiments for a small, rural radio station! The university secured a Rockefeller Foundation grant to send their new station manager to the United States on a three month educational tour of leading radio stations. He spent one month observing the operational and production methods of NBC's Radio City. He studied the broadcast business at Columbia University's Office of Radio Research and at the universities of Ohio State, Iowa, and Wisconsin. He examined the work of the Rocky Mountain Radio Council in Colorado and visited the CBS studios in Chicago.

He travelled by train. Airflight was as new a technology as radio. My father apparently had no problem being 'on' the air but he was nervous of being 'in' the air.

When CJFX in Antigonish hit the airwaves, Catholic radio buffs noted the irony of that date, the holy Feast of the Annunciation. The radio programs on CJFX were to complement the university's outreach programs, to teach economic self-sufficiency and the co-operative movement philosophy that was by then famous. Kitchen study clubs were held in rural areas, study outlines and questionnaires were sent out in advance, and the fishermen and farmer listening groups huddled together, following along panel discussions heard on the kitchen radio. It was a 'University of the Air' for non-traditional students studying off campus. It was part of the heady buzz in the educational movement of the day, bringing the classroom to the people.

Those CJFX radio programs had names such as "People's School," "Farmer's Forum," "Life in These Maritimes," and "Nova Scotia Labour Forum."

University Professors and other experts joined the panels and the new station manager—the only panelist with radio experience—was usually the moderator.

The old tapes of those 1940s programs make for quite a study in old broadcast speaking style. And the show content was pretty practical stuff.

Here's an excerpt of Nunn's introduction to one program:

"Good evening ladies and gentlemen, this is 'Life in These Maritimes.' Tonight on 'Life in These Maritimes' we have another broadcast on the current series dealing with the farmer's woodlot. Tonight, specifically, we are talking about pulpwood, its future and yours. On the panel, as you have just heard, we have Gordon MacRae and Tom Chisholm, members of the executive of the Atlantic Forest Products Cooperative, and Bernie MacLellan, field worker for Cape Breton Cooperative Services. Now I am sure all of you are keenly aware of the campaign that's been going on for the establishment of a pulp mill somewhere in the Strait of Canso area… I'd like to ask either of you, perhaps you, ah, Tom how the individual woodlot owner feels about the possibilities of this mill becoming…"

Well! A listener would have to be seriously committed to the topic to stay tuned! But it is arguably comparable to pressing pulp issues you might hear 'panelized' on CBC's respected "Maritime Noon" program today. The resource issues haven't changed much, and some Nova Scotians' livelihoods hang in the balance today as they did back then. Nevertheless, some programs in the early years of CJFX were a far cry from 'easy listening' radio. But then, I wasn't born yet so who am I to say?

Want another broadcasting blast from the past? Another announcer introduced "People's School" this way:

"Good Afternoon ladies and gentlemen, this is 'People's School.' Today we bring you the first panel discussion in the 1954-55 series of 'People's School.' The topic to be discussed is: What's ahead for the Canadian Economy? Guests on the program are…"

You have to give them credit. It wasn't the mind mush we hear so much of today on private stations. But it probably couldn't compete with the Much Music/World Wide Web attention spans, now would it?

But variety was the spice of CJFX life. As a CBC affiliate, it offered world news. I first heard the CBC on CJFX. Its program mix boasted both classical and Celtic music, and both political and religious talk. There were tips on canning vegetables and other "women's" features. Zita Cameron's program taught how to organize adult study clubs. Sister Marie Michael's program discussed good books to read. The core staff was so small, even the secretary had 15 minutes of fame, playing records on a program called Today's Tunes. After an office romance that didn't escape the notice of staff members, Nora McKenna later became the station manager's wife. And I oughta know—that's how I came to be here! My seven siblings too.

This unique radio venture was operated as a separate company, Atlantic Broadcasters Limited. It sold shares. But it also sold airtime for radio commercials. That's where the much-loved and listened to program "Fun At Five" came in. It was pure, sponsored entertainment that paid the bills. Rural listeners throughout Antigonish, Guysborough, Pictou, and the Cape Breton counties—even the east end of Prince Edward Island—made it a daily radio ritual.

"Fun At Five" became a fixture for 25 years in that end of the province. Hosted by that same station manager, Clyde Nunn, who altered his voice to take on the speech and character of 'The Oldtimer,' a stereotype of the craggy country hayseed. His sidekick was a talkative fisherman named Percy Baker, whose genuine Maritime accent and rural language were just as country-bumpkin sounding as The Oldtimer's fake voice. With his crude guitar playing and nasal singing, Percy made for a fine foil for The Oldtimer's on-air wit, whether Percy was always aware of it or not! This odd couple made for a fun pair live on the air. Every night at

CJFX Radio staff: J.C. Nunn, centre rear; Nora Nunn, seated, centre right.

five. (This, before the CBC's popular rural send-up, the Rawhide program with Max Ferguson.)

Yes, "Fun At Five" always brought a smile. Even today, I still see its mere mention causes old CJFX listeners to grin in amusement. For many hard-working people, the show was a rewarding bit of witty silliness and 'Scotch' music at the end of the day's labours. The program opened with the catchy war-time tune, "Pack Up Your Troubles."

Here's how the opening sounded with The Oldtimer and Percy on the 25th anniversary program in 1968.

(music fades under voice…)

OLDTIMER: Hello folks, Hellooo and how ya's all gettin' along this evenin' and a how? By gum, we ah, we finally got in here. I come in all dressed up, put on the new jumper and the new overalls, polished up the old barn boots and they let us come in the backdoor. And I mean by us, old Percy and me.

(A little banter follows in their thick Maritime accents and then a reference to Percy's alleged moonshine making.)

OLDTIMER:…I suppose we're lucky to get in a-tall, the way we look. I got the chores done pretty early. You got a mash a brewin' you told me.

PERCY: Ahh, my gracious me (Percy leaves it at that.)

Maybe The Oldtimer was on to something there?

They reminisce about previous jokes they shared over the years, including reference to Percy the moonshine-maker giving the RCMP— "Them fellas with the yellow stripes down their pants and the boy scout hats"—a run for their money.

Percy laughs it off. Then The Oldtimer redirects with some personal pokes, just for fun.

OLDTIMER: Well, now Percy let me talk to ya. When did you start broadcasting on CJFX?

PERCY: A few months or so after the station opened, I think September of the same year, I come on the rattio.

OLDTIMER: You did? That was first mistake we made! That wasn't the first but it was one of the big ones. Then the second was keepin' ya on for 25 years!

That was their act. At some point Percy would play his twangy guitar (The Oldtimer called it Percy's 'weapon') and sing "The Pride of Glencoe" or some similar traditional tune. Back then, Nova Scotians for miles around loved the program. It was a marked contrast from the earlier years when educational, economic, and religious programming also ran at other times of the broadcast day, moderated by Nunn in his real voice. When radio was in its infancy, you could get away with things like that.

CJFX station in Antigonish: an early radio experiment.

In one classic Oldtimer/Percy story, the Oldtimer innocently asked Percy, the fisherman, if he ever had a leak in the boat.

Percy replied, either genuinely or with cunning wit, "No, I always made it to shore in time."

The Oldtimer didn't get it. He pressed on with the program. Even after leaving the downtown studio, he was befuddled by Main Street merchants laughing when they saw him. As I heard the story, my mother had to explain it to him when he got home. Percy had got the better of him!

Another day, Nunn came from a university dinner table discussion on campus about a new breakthrough in science: jet-propulsion. He hurried up the station stairs for the live "Fun At Five" program. As The Oldtimer, he told his listening audience how this newfangled science worked to help him and Percy get into town. He described how they threw turnips off the back of his wagon to propel the horse and cart forward faster! I'm told it was some time before the laughter subsided around the priestly professors' dinner table where they were listening to the broadcast.

Some radio listeners were sure The Oldtimer was a real person talking specifically to them. One day The Oldtimer warned listeners to watch that the bread baking in the oven didn't burn. A woman wrote in later asking in astonishment how the old man could have possibly known that she was making bread that day! Other listeners sent in homemade knitted goods and other gifts to The Oldtimer. Perhaps some new socks for those cold barn boots?

Trusting fans such as those were unaware that it was the station manager behind that curmudgeonly voice. He was shocked when one listener as far away as Newfoundland generously sent him, by mail, a gift of fresh fish! Well, it was fresh when it was mailed, at least. Imagine the scene in the station when that package was opened!

CJFX included many St.F.X. students learning the ropes of radio. Celtic performer John Allen Cameron credits Nunn's influence with his launch into performing. Cameron not only worked at the station, occasionally singing on air, he apparently slept in the building. Senators Ernie Finlay MacDonald and Al Graham shaped their public speaking talents there. As did Terry MacLellan, later a popular TV personality and Cape Breton promoter.

Hockey's celebrated play-by-play announcer Danny Gallivan did his early sports broadcasts at CJFX. Gallivan's college roommate was Danny Petrie, now a Hollywood movie mogul. Petrie credits CJFX and his cousin Clyde Nunn with launching him onto his show business path in the United States by introducing him to a course in New York on the new medium called television. The Oldtimer went into provincial politics in the 1950s, served as Minister of Welfare and spent nine years representing the people of Inverness County.

CJFX Radio was, and is, an institution in the cultural fabric of that primarily rural, Celtic corner of the province. But its educational side dwindled with the advent of TV, and with changing times and technology. Dr. Coady passed away in 1959 and the university naturally showed less interest in the old radio outreach concept. It was perhaps an expected evolution. But, my! How the spirit of that exciting new thing called radio had captured the imaginations of Nova Scotia's greatest adult educators. They saw it as a chance to do some good. And for a few years, a noble educational experiment was conducted on the airwaves of this province.

Biplane Bicatch

A Nova Scotian schooner responds
to drowning airmen in wartime waters.

I t was an odd coincidence and a Nova Scotian schooner that saved the
life of a British biplane pilot in 1944. Today, eighty-year-old John
Godley, also known as Lord Kilbracken, is a retired member of the
British House of Lords, a war veteran and author living in County
Cavan, Ireland. But in May of '44, he was a young Royal Airforce pilot
escorting a convoy of ships across the Atlantic to Halifax and New York.
He was in the air, about three hundred miles off our coast, patrolling
for enemy U-boats, when trouble struck.

By telephone, from his old, stone, Irish mansion, Godley described
his plane for me.

"We were flying the very ancient-looking Fairey Swordfish biplane
aircraft," he said in the leather-patches-and-pipe accent you might
stereotypically expect of an old British Lord telling war stories. "A mass
of struts and wires and so on. It had two wings, a fixed undercarriage, a
fixed pitch prop and a top speed of about a hundred."

They were known, in slang, as Stringbags. That's why Godley's
autobiography is called *Bring Back My Stringbag: Swordfish Pilot at War
1940-1945*.

Flying far south from his convoy, Godley and his crew of two were
shocked to see a fishing boat below. "We couldn't understand what this
schooner was doing way out in the Atlantic with U-boats around," he said.

They joked that maybe it was the *Marie Celeste*, the mysterious Nova
Scotian ghost ship found drifting in 1872.

Just then, they spotted another rarity. Another biplane from the
convoy, flying in the distance. The odds of that chance meeting over the
vast Atlantic were very slim.

"A minute after that I lost all power," said the veteran pilot. "There was no warning. There was no stuttering of the engine or coughing or faltering; just a clean cut of the engine."

Perhaps he ran out of petrol, though the gauge didn't show it.

Gliding down, attempting to restart the engine, Godley fired off all eight metal-piercing rockets to lighten the load and hopefully signal the schooner. The plane then ditched easily in the cold Atlantic, far from the warm Gulf Stream.

The schooner, twelve miles away, didn't notice the downed plane. The fishermen were working over the far side of the vessel. The other biplane in the air tried to alert the fishing crew to what was happening. Diving and dropping smoke cannisters over the crash site, the airborne plane then flashed useless Morse code signals at the bewildered fishermen.

Unsure and worried, the fishermen "went down below and found a Canadian flag (the old red ensign) and spread this out on the quarter deck because they thought this airplane was trying to establish whether they were friend or foe."

Finally realizing the crisis, the schooner crew sailed toward the downed biplane. Surviving almost an hour in the frigid ocean water, the three airmen were barely alive, hanging from a single one-man dinghy in rolling waves.

"It was bloody cold," said Godley. "I lost consciousness as we were lifted out of the water by the crew of the fishing vessel."

The airman had held on just long enough. Once in the rescuers' arms, he allowed himself to pass out.

But the young pilot was in for one more fright. "When I came to, which was nearly an hour later, I

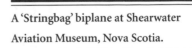

A 'Stringbag' biplane at Shearwater Aviation Museum, Nova Scotia.

was surrounded by husky sailors all speaking German! I thought I must have been picked up by a U-Boat," he said.

Imagine his shock. But soon he understood. They were Nova Scotian fishermen out of Lunenburg, a place settled by German families two centuries ago. The Germanic accent was still detectable.

The *Kasagra* was their vessel, a small, sixty-foot schooner. Her captain, Atwood Parks, and his crew poured whiskey into the near-drowned British airmen, carefully and slowly warming their frigid bodies. The men were later picked up by their convoy, put on a hospital ship, and taken into Halifax Harbour where they stayed at the naval base on the Dartmouth side for a few days, recovering.

And for dropping his fishing lines and responding to save this aircrew's lives, Captain Atwood Parks of East LaHave was honoured with the distinction of membership in the Order of the British Empire.

Captain Parks didn't attend the ceremony in Ottawa because he was busy fishing. A medal was sent to him. The memory of what that Nova Scotian vessel *Kasagra* did is not buried. Fifty-seven years later, John Godley, the Irish Lord, is still grateful.

"We were absolutely at the limit of endurance when the boats were lowered and we were picked out of the water," he said, "She saved our lives, there's no doubt about that whatsoever."

Pilot John Godley, centre, and his crew of two: rescued just in time.

Final words: Captain Parks' grandson Barry Parks approached me to explain that his grandfather actually spoke English but, like many Lunenburgers, he still spoke with German expressions and inflections, enough to startle the groggy, awakening pilot. Also, inspired by hearing his grandfather's story told on radio, Barry arranged for a new permanent display about this biplane bicatch at Lunenburg's Fisheries Museum of the Atlantic. His grandfather's prestigious medal, though, he is keeping, close to his heart and within the Parks family, a reminder of the great saga of *Kasagra*.

The Man Who Made Bluenose

How a soda pop bottler drew magic into the Bluenose blueprints.

T all ships ahoy! A forest of wooden masts sashed in billowing white sails; that's the wonderful scene thousands of visitors eagerly anticipated while lining the sides of Halifax Harbour in the summer of 2000. I was one of them, sitting with my two young boys on the edge of a Halifax pier. We all wanted one thing. A voyage back in time to the era of great, glorious, majestic wooden ships. And no such beautiful vessel better represented that golden era in Nova Scotia than our own nostalgically iconographic schooner—the original *Bluenose*. May she rest in peace.

Her legacy—reborn in *Bluenose Two*—holds strong in our hearts and in our history. Her life story was so magical it's as if she were meant to be, as if she were meant to excel in glory, racing us to a level of poignant pride and particular self-identity just before the decline of the mighty fishing schooner era.

We were known as Bluenoses to American traders and so in rebellious irony we gave that nickname to the schooner we built to beat them in the International Fisherman's Trophy Races of the 1920s and 30s. The original *Bluenose* was fastest in the world for almost twenty years and retired undefeated.

Sure it was the wily Captain Angus Walters and his hardened crew that pulled it off. But before her hull met water, before her bowsprit crossed the first finish line, intellect, intuition, talent, and spirit were infused into the famous schooner's design.

There was magic in those *Bluenose* blueprints. The magician was William J. (Bill) Roué, a self-taught naval architect.

Like Churchill, Bill Roué came along at just the right time in Nova Scotia's war for schooner racing domination. Angus Walters wanted a ship precisely crafted to speed through wind and wave, cutting seconds off sailing times wherever possible.

Roué was seemingly an odd choice of nautical designer for this serious project: a man who came very late to naval architecture and without formal training. He had never designed such a fishing schooner before. Despite requiring a razor-sharp knowledge of efficient movement through water, he didn't even know how to swim. He was to give the world its fastest schooner!

It doesn't seem right somehow. But appearances are as deceptive as a red sky in morning at sea. William J. Roué had a natural knack. "He started as early as the age of four," said Joan Roué, "whittling boats from pieces of wood."

Joan is the great-granddaughter of the *Bluenose* designer. She agrees that her great grandfather seemed to get his gift from nowhere, without a family influence. "His father wasn't into boats," she told me. "His Dad owned Roué Carbonated Waters, a pop manufacturing company."

Bill Roué took over the company from his father. He was a bottler. Now, I

Parts of schooner *Bluenose* were designed in a soda pop factory. Really!

know how they get those little ship's models into bottles but how the heck do you get a model for a ship out of a bottler? Simply put, he really wasn't a bottler. His heart wasn't in it. His true calling was to mathematically breathe life and grace into well-cut sailing vessels.

Drawing boats was his real love. After all, he had doodled his way through school. "They say it was born in him," said Joan.

He must have been struck by watching the dance of sails in the harbour of his boyhood. His father's bottling plant was in the Collins Building at present day Historic Properties on the Halifax waterfront. Later, Roué lived in the house high atop Dartmouth's James Street hill, on the corner at

Summit, which afforded a good view of the harbour waters before the trees grew tall.

"So he was on the harbour and around boats all the time," said Joan. "It was in him. It was a passion."

Through the eyes of babes. Something about boats must have caught Bill Roué's young fancy and was lashed tightly there for the rest of his life's voyage.

He doodled and drew, read boat books by the bundle, and learned on his own. He bottled by day and drew *Bluenose* by night.

With the reputation earned from his first, famous schooner, Roué retired from bottling to just draw ships. From his big wooden drafting table, a variety of original floating creations flowed forth on paper to become reality on water: The celebrated line of Roué Class sailing boats, car ferries, even wartime landing craft.

He tried a stint with a big nautical design firm in New York. While there, he actually attempted to create a new schooner that could beat his own *Bluenose*. His design was built into a vessel called *Halifax*. But not even the magician who blew life into Bluenose could reverse her spell. She remained on top.

Her sister, *Bluenose Two*, led the tall ships' parade of sail in graceful sweeps under blue skies down Halifax Harbour. The crowd—and the boys—loved it.

The Tragedy of the Lost Patrol

The Public Gardens link to a northern Mountie's heroic end.

I n the pleasant Public Gardens of Halifax, behind the elegant wrought-iron gates, amid the flourish of flowers and splashing ducks on warm summer days, there is a symbol of tragedy and heroism in Canada's frigid far north.

It's a charming little bridge that gently arches over a stream but also spans time to past events—harsh, horrible events. The bridge and its plaque, dated 1911, were built to honour the courageous Inspector Francis J. Fitzgerald of the infamous Lost Patrol.

Fitzgerald was born on Halifax's Hollis street. In 1885, at age 16, he went north with the Halifax Battalion at the time of the North West Rebellion. As a member of the Royal North West Mounted Police (R.N.W.M.P.), Fitzgerald was leading a routine, annual patrol of men from Fort MacPherson in the North West Territories to Dawson City, Yukon, about a thousand miles. His group had three sleds and fifteen dogs.

Barbara Hinds was touched by Fitzgerald's story and put it to paper in her book called *The Lost Patrol*. In it, she quotes from Fitzgerald's journal, written during that brutal trek in the bitter winter of 1910-11.

"Sunday: 64 below," he wrote. "Fine with strong headwind. Left camp at 8:30 and only made one drive. Slow going with intense cold. 9 miles today."

Clearly, it was a far cry from the lovely Victorian Public Gardens of his home city in Nova Scotia.

Fitzgerald's group was travelling light, perhaps too light. Their dogs were not properly rested before leaving. And the snow was three feet deep along the frozen rivers.

Trouble arrived a week into their journey. They had missed the trail for Dawson. They hired a native named Esau who guided them for five days but then they let him go. Fitzgerald trusted one of his men named Carter who said he could take them the rest of the way. But in frigid conditions they soon learned poor Carter was wrong. They were lost. Their dogs were exhausted. They wasted food and energy searching up one creek then another.

Fitzgerald writes that he "should not have taken Carter's word that he knew the way from Little Wind River."

The men suffered. Their feet ballooned out and cracked with frostbite. Their scant provisions dwindled to nothing. They were forced to gradually eat their sole means of transport.

"We killed another dog today…We have only five left," Fitzgerald writes.

The dogs were thin and sickly. Their meat made the men sick but kept them alive. Desperate, they turned around to head back to Fort MacPherson but things looked bleak and foreboding.

In his last journal entry, the inspector writes, "Just after noon I broke through the ice and had to make a fire. Found one foot slightly frozen. Killed another dog tonight. Can only go a few miles a day. Everybody breaking out on the body and skin peeling off. 8 miles today."

Two constables succumbed to frostbite. Fitzgerald and Carter left them behind, barely alive but wrapped in the groups' sleeping furs. The two men left standing pressed on with just half a blanket each to sleep in. A cold death was certain.

Later, the leader of a search party—Inspector Dempster—wrote in his journal that when he found the two men, Carter had died first and Fitzgerald had laid him out, a handkerchief over his face.

Knowing he would soon be gone too, Inspector Fitzgerald laid down by his small fire. "He wrote his will," said Ms. Hinds, "scratched out with the end of a burnt stick from his fire."

Gardens' bridge dedicated to great Canadian northern hero.

She first saw the crude will, written on a crumpled paper, on display in a small log cabin museum in the Yukon. It reads: "All money in despatch bag and bank, clothes, etc., I leave to my dearly beloved mother, Mrs. John Fitzgerald, Halifax. God Bless All. F. J. Fitzgerald, R. N. W. M. P."

Fitzgerald kept his faculties and emotions in focus to the frozen end. Knowing he was doomed, this early Canadian Mountie made his dying men comfortable and trudged on against all odds. When he knew all was lost, his last thought was to provide for his mother.

No wonder he was hailed a hero across the country. The Public Gardens commission cemented his place in history with that pretty bridge in his name.

Now here's a modern-day twist to the story. I spoke to a Mr. Thomas Spearns of Halifax who had a great grandmother who was a Fitzgerald.

He told me this story was oft talked about in his family. Mr. Spearns was inspired to a life as a Halifax police officer. Now retired from the force, he gives tours of the city's Public Gardens. He always stops at the small bridge to tell tourists about the brave Inspector Fitzgerald and the lost patrol.

Surgical Survival

Bluenose surgeon performs pioneer kidney transplant.

Imagine the anxious excitement of surgeons the first time they removed a kidney from a healthy human to install the organ in a much weaker patient dying of kidney disease. It happened in Canada 43 years ago for the first time in all the British commonwealth countries. The surgical pioneer was from Mahoney's Beach, Antigonish County: Dr. Ken MacKinnon.

A Dalhousie Medical School graduate, MacKinnon has resettled by the shore in his retirement. At eighty, he looks back on a long medical career teaching at McGill University and operating at the Royal Victoria Hospital in Montreal where this medical milestone was made, May 14, 1958.

A teenage girl arrived in emergency. She was convulsing. She was down to just five percent kidney function—likely the fall-out from a long-forgotten childhood infection. Moira Johnson was in serious trouble. But she had a twin sister, Nola, who volunteered her own healthy, left kidney. The first kidney transplant in the world had been attempted only a few years earlier in Boston. So the girl's only hope was for a doctor to go there, learn the techniques, return and attempt a transplant.

Dr. MacKinnon was chosen. But time was short.

"At that particular period there wasn't going to be an alternative," said Dr. MacKinnon when I reached him at his home. "It wasn't too many years later chronic dialysis would have become possible so I guess we knew that either this was going to work or she was going to die."

MacLean's Magazine (July 16, 1960) gave the story five pages, calling the surgery a "chilling gamble." Two surgical rooms were set up. Dr. MacKinnon was a co-leader of a surgical team. He made the incision, extracted the healthy kidney from the donor and that's when the clock started counting down for him.

They didn't know how long they could safely deprive a healthy organ of its arterial blood flow. "We knew that in the Boston experience the time was up around an hour or a little bit under so we wanted to make sure we weren't longer than that," he said. "I guess we were about 58 minutes…of arterial deprivation."

The bold surgery was also a 'first' in medical ethics. A special court order was required even though the parents and the underage donor were agreeable. Removing a healthy organ went against the doctor's training.

Dr. MacKinnon struggled with that issue. "I didn't like that," he said. "I found that disturbing. When you are dealing with someone with no illness, well, I guess there was more anxiety because of this new experience."

An American medical ethicist openly criticized the surgeons for violating Judeo-Christian values. This was some time before the Pope himself gave his blessing to transplants. Dr. MacKinnon and his fellows were in an ethical no-man's land. But they had no other option. The patient was very weak.

Yet, although the sisters were twins, who knew if the transplant would "take"? It was pioneering surgery, new to the Montreal doctors, new to the country.

The moment of truth came. Dr. MacKinnon replaced the girl's failing kidney with the new healthy organ. The connection to the artery was completed with the technical assistance of another Nova Scotian surgeon, Dr. Norman Beliveau, a graduate of St. Anne's College from Beliveau Cove, Digby County.

The stressful surgery took three hours but one breath-holding moment was pivotal. "When the clamps were taken off the artery, the kidney just lit up," said MacKinnon, "in terms of changing colour from

Dr. Ken MacKinnon: celebrated urine drops at first kidney transplant!

a dark colour to the normal sort of bright, reddish-brown colour."

That brightness showed "that the kidney was profusing satisfactorily."

"It was really very dramatic to see the change," he said, "I think we were all very excited."

But then, another crucial hurdle. Would the new organ not only thrive but also function properly? Again, suspense.

Then, relief!

"When we first observed drops of urine coming out of the ureter," said MacKinnon, "slowly at first then speeding up, those were the two most exciting things. It was great!"

"We were all pretty excited," said the retired surgeon.

Celebrating drops of urine! If ever there was a time, that was it: success!

Dr. MacKinnon later gave medical papers on the pioneering transplant all over—as far as Scotland where he showed a film of the operation. His medical career continued in Montreal, then later overseas and, for a while, in Halifax before the doctor resettled in Antigonish County.

The twins lived normal lives. Both held jobs at *Reader's Digest* in Montreal and remained very close all their lives. The kidney recipient, Moira Johnson, lived 25 more years until kidney failure unexpectedly crept in again. But her sister Nola, the organ donor, is well and about to retire. Near the time we talked, Dr. MacKinnon told me he had heard from a mutual medical friend that Nola and her mother look back with good feelings on all that happened. They believe it was a meaningful survival for all concerned.

A good life was lived.

And for a former surgeon living seaside now, good memories live too.

Polar Bears, Monkeys, and Moose

First North American zoo, right here!

Before New York, before Boston, Halifax was first to have a zoo. It's true, a zoo! Imagine a menagerie of strange, exotic animals in the woods a couple of blocks up Halifax's busy Dutch Village Road from the traffic-heavy Armdale Rotary. Well, it's not there anymore. But in the 1850s and 1860s beasts and critters filled the one hundred acres of treed property on the edge of the old city. A piece of the zookeeper's paradise still remains as a privately-owned, untouched sanctuary in the city.

A self-taught naturalist of the highest order, our pioneering zookeeper Andrew Downs came to Halifax from New Jersey with his family when he was fourteen years old. His father was in the plumbing business, but Andrew was a born naturalist. He loved animals and birds, alive and otherwise. His zoological gardens offered displays of beautiful birds and fascinating creatures, both living and stuffed. Visitors came from all over Nova Scotia and from across the Atlantic.

Shirley Hill, whose family is only the third owner of the former zoo site, allowed me a tour of the pretty property. Her archival research tells her that Downs' zoo featured an "aviary, an aquarium and a museum of stuffed birds."

"It was the first zoological garden in North America north of Mexico," she said, and the federal government plaque on the monument next to the street supports her claim.

The aviary, known as the 'glass house,' was a building made of wood and glass featuring a tall tower for rare tropical birds. It stood on a crag overlooking a meandering stream. From its top, long before the trees grew tall and buildings obstructed the view, a visitor's vista stretched across the city to Citadel Hill and out over Halifax Harbour. Today, the wooded area surrounding Downs' former home has trees "a hundred or so feet tall, many untouched all this time."

Over the years, Mr. Downs' zoological gardens were home to South American ducks, a crane from Mississippi, a variety of domestic fowl and wild birds, Californian quails, bald headed eagles in a cage, and even free-range moose roaming the surrounding woods. Downs shipped mooseheads to buyers around the world. He also kept elk, wolves, foxes, deer, beaver, and even a monkey.

"In the pond he had seals, otter, mink, and a polar bear in the lower pond," said Hill.

A polar bear in Nova Scotia?

Yup. Shipped by steamer, down from Labrador, it was!

In Victorian days, "visitors came out by steamer and by coach and carriage up from the head of the North West Arm. They came for afternoon picnics," said Hill. Back then, it would have been a lovely day's excursion from the inner-city to the countryside. On one anniversary of Halifax, a thousand people travelled out there to enjoy the zoological gardens.

Treed site of first zoo north of Mexico, marked by monument in Halifax.

Downs was a highly respected taxidermist. One report says he stuffed eight hundred mooseheads for buyers at home and abroad. He received exhibition awards from London, Dublin and Paris.

Even the famous flocked to see Downs' feathered friends. King Victor Emmanuel of Italy and the Prince of Wales (later King Edward VII of England) came to the zoo. A writer from *Field and Stream* and a representative of the Smithsonian Institution in Washington also came to call.

When New York City opened its zoo many years after Downs had his up and running, they offered our zookeeper the position of superintendent of the menagerie. So, according to former archivist Bruce Ferguson, Downs sold his beautiful land and animals and moved his family to New York.

But he lasted there only three months.

"There was a misunderstanding or disagreement and he came back to Halifax," said Hill.

He tried to establish a new zoo, just south of his old property, but it failed. Although this lover of nature ended up living in the city's centre, on Agricola Street, he still kept feathered creatures around him.

"He was totally involved with his birds and his poultry," said Hill. "He never lost that love; it was his life."

Today, Andrew Downs' old home still stands on the former zoo site minus its elegant Victorian gables. It's still called Walton Cottage, a name he chose after Walton Hall, the home of his mentor, a respected British naturalist. The neighbourhood boasts a Walton Drive and Downs Avenue, a few remaining reminders of the unusual attraction that once was there.

Amongst the tall trees straddling the stream, the occasional chastising chatter of city squirrels can be heard, but the exotic roars and screeches of North America's first zoo are lost in the distant past.

Cɪʋɪl Wαɾ Sυɾʋeɥοɾ

Bluenose Yankee kept best war diary ever found.

"One [civil war historian] *said it's the most important civil war document since the memoirs of General U.S. Grant."*
—Dr. Charles Bryan, Director Virginia Historical Society, Richmond, Virginia, U.S.A.

Now that's unique! Especially since the document writer was a civil war veteran from Annapolis Royal, Nova Scotia. Obsessively detailed, the memoir was based on in-the-field diaries (close to five thousand pages) and includes about eight hundred well-rendered sketches and maps of battle fields, war camps, and prisons. One hundred and forty years old, it was discovered, edited and published for the first time by Dr. Charles Bryan and Nelson Lankford.

Private Robert Knox Sneden (pronounced Snee-den) was the wartime writer. Descended from New York Loyalists who settled in Nova Scotia in the 1780s, Sneden's parents married at St. Paul's Church in Halifax. He called himself an engineer and architectural draftsman. "We think he had a good solid education in the Canadian school system," said Bryan. Sneden's memoir contains "frequent references to ancient and military history, throwing in quotes from French."

His family moved to New York just before the Civil War broke out, when Sneden was 18. He signed up with the 40th New York Regiment of the Union army.

He gives a ground-level view in words and pictures of several Civil War battles of the 1860s: from Malvern Hill near Richmond to the infamous Battle of Bull Run. He describes "the roar of the cannon and the shrieks of the Confederate troops on the other side of the line; the shrieks of the dying and wounded."

Sneden was very graphic, describing every gruesome detail. "He walks back to his tent," said Bryan, " and there's blood spattered all over the place and there are flies and it smells awful."

Sneden sent his descriptions back to his home to be worked on later. He was curious. He toured about the war camps and towns, observing and recording everything. "As a mapmaker, he would go up on the front lines exposing himself to enemy fire," said Bryan. "He came close more than once to being killed."

"During the siege of York town," said Bryan, "he's out between the lines and a Confederate battery sights him."

Suddenly, he's under fire! "He describes jumping under trees and in ditches, running back to the Union lines!"

He became privy to important war information when his commander was seconded to Washington and took Sneden with him. Then followed a year of soft living: theatre, dining, and a warm bed while he worked on war maps.

But in 1863, Sneden was sent back into battle and was captured by John Mosby, the Gray Ghost of the Confederacy.

He barely survived a horrendous year in the infamous, crowded and disease-ridden Andersonville Prison in the south. There, he kept up his war diary on scraps of paper he hid in his shoes, and sewed into his clothes.

Sneden was very proud of his Nova Scotian roots.

While in prison in 1864, a man asked him if he was a Yankee. Of that, Sneden writes this: "I told him I was a Bluenose from Nova Scotia but had lived much at New York." (Note he does not use 'Bluenoser,' a recent distortion of Nova Scotians' original, proper nickname.)

Sneden regaled his prison guards with tales of "moose hunting, salmon and herring fishing, wild geese shooting, etc., as we practice them in Nova Scotia."

Nova Scotian Robert Sneden's frontlines sketch of an American Civil War battle.

He writes, "Although not one of them ever heard of such a country, they were interested and even volunteered to shoot over my head in case they would be detailed for my execution."

How nice. Lucky for him, he never did go before the firing squad.

Sneden also recalls in his memoir the time a Sargent Wells of Halifax died; the four other Bluenoses also in his New York regiment paid for Wells' coffin. These Nova Scotians were among almost fifty thousand Canadians who fought in that American war for one reason or another.

When war ended, Sneden remained without a wife or much success in his working life. He poured himself into his huge album of drawings and diary notes from the battlefield.

"It was obvious," said Bryan, "that the Civil War was burned in his memory. It was the defining experience of his existence on the earth and he spent year after year transcribing his Civil War diary into this memoir, a true chronicle of a remarkable man's experience at war."

Civil War artist R. K. Sneden of Annapolis Royal.

He died alone in a home for ex-sailors in Bath New York in 1918.

For about eighty years, Private Robert K. Sneden's memoir, maps, and drawings were kept by relatives in different parts of the United States.

A few years ago, a relative brought the drawings to the attention of historians in Virginia. Through the kind of complex, investigative hunt that I've grown accustomed to, the historians found the memoir and published much of Sneden's work under the title *Eye of the Storm—A Civil War Odyssey*.

It's a unique, eye-opening, eyewitness account of America's greatest inner siege. They can thank that Bluenose boy from Annapolis Royal.

"He brings it alive unlike anything I had ever read," said Bryan.

Remembering the Fuller Brush Man

Local farm boy makes big bucks from brushes.

I still remember my mother opening the door to a smiling, smartly dressed salesman with a big leather case. It was a sunny Saturday morning. He flipped open the display case flaps on the kitchen table, unveiling an array of new bristle brushes, all shapes and lengths, the handles smoothly formed. The Fuller Brush Man was a household name. As a kid, I didn't know then that he was one of seven thousand door-to-door brush salesmen who rang 140 million door bells a year for the multi-million dollar, international Fuller Brush Company. And that all that bristling success began in a simple farmer's field in Annapolis Valley.

Alfred Carl Fuller was a big, hard-working, uneducated farmhand born in Welsford, King's County. As the original Fuller Brush Man, once called the greatest travelling salesman in the world, he lived a literal rags to riches story.

In his 1960 autobiography, *A Foot in the Door*, he writes that his idea of employing "independent dealers who are businessmen in their own communities, draw no salary from the company, and earn only the fruits of their own sales, was germinated in a Nova Scotia strawberry patch."

He endured hard, hot farm labour as a boy. He learned to make brushes from his brother Dwight, who made and sold the hog hair bristle brushes as a sideline in Boston. When Dwight died of tuberculosis in 1901, his business partner, William Staples, took a young Alfred Fuller under his wing and taught him how to fashion the hog hair and wire brushes, to pack his salesman's case properly, and to approach customers, primarily housewives.

In the beginning, constant rejection at the door was no problem.

"Eighteen years of rugged Nova Scotia farm life," writes Fuller, "had made me impervious to discouragement."

Fuller knocked on dozens of doors a day in the 1910-1920 era. Once he got his foot in the door, he began to see a whole new niche market: customized cleaning brushes.

He split from William Staples and began making his own special kinds of brushes: long handled ones for dusting high ceiling moldings, curved brushes to fit into glass tops on oil lamps, even long, narrow brushes to clean behind old iron radiators.

Hardworking housewives loved them. So Fuller moved to Hartford, Connecticut to open his own company.

The Fuller Brush Man was on his way.

His book title hints at the slick salesman stereotype. But Fuller's grand nephew Earl Fuller in the valley, his granddaughter in Halifax, and his relatives in the United States all told me when I phoned them that they remember Alfred Fuller as a generous, kind, religious man. He ran his life and his company by the Good Book.

Bill Skerrett, an independent documentary maker in Dartmouth who researched Fuller's life for History Television, agrees the Fuller Brush Man wasn't pushy.

"Contrary to the belief," said Skerrett, "his philosophy was when the housewife opened the door he stepped back, not forward. He didn't put his foot in the door."

The greatest travelling salesman in the world was shy!

Door-to-door sales rang in. The company's reputation preceded each doorbell chime. Eventually, the Fuller Brush Man was overtaken by the Fuller Brush Woman!

"Alfred's first wife actually outsold him two to one," said Bill. "He ended up staying at home making the brushes and she ended up out there making sales."

The Fuller business got fuller.

From his famous brushes came brushes with fame.

Two movies were made: one called *The Fuller Brush Man* starring Red Skelton, the other was *The Fuller Brush Woman* featuring Lucille Ball.

Then came a brush with power. When he had a scheduled meeting with the American president, a newspaper cartoon showed Fuller with his foot in the door of the White House.

He had made it!

But he also shared his bristling wealth. Alfred Fuller, the unschooled country bumpkin, founded the University of Hartford's very reputable music school.

In time, the Fuller Brush empire was handed over to Alfred's sons, then sold off. From an initial 375 dollar investment, the modern company is now worth about 400 million.

That's a lot of hog hair.

Alfred Carl Fuller died a wealthy man in 1973. His gravesite is in his Nova Scotian hometown, Welsford. His 'how to sell' recordings are ensconced in our public archives in Halifax. And the summer house in Yarmouth, which he shared with his second wife, Primrose Pelton, is now a museum.

The Fuller Brush legacy is a great one: From farmer's field to fame and fortune.

⌁⌁⌁⌁⌁

Sally Anne Starts Here

By mistake or mystique,
the Salvationist spirit came ashore.

Pioneering preaching in Nova Scotia's harbour city—Salvationist style! We had it and we had it first. The Salvation Army's invasion of Canada began with a battle for souls in Halifax of 1881. That's one year before the Sally Anne's official Canadian invasion of Upper Canada. Why were we first in Sally Anne-dom? Actually, it was an accident, or perhaps divine intervention: When the Salvation Army's first commissioner—a man of great oratory and energy, George Scott Railton—stepped ashore here, he didn't mean to stay.

Railton was a Scot, sent from London, England to New York as a pioneer of the new religious movement. But he was soon recalled to London Headquarters. On his way back, his steamer stopped in Halifax, as steamers on that route often did.

Railton wandered from the docked ship into the dirty streets of the old navy town. There, he was inspired to do something completely spontaneous.

An 86-year-old retired general of the holy Army, General Arnold Brown has collected this history.

"The Commissioner felt compelled to stand at one of the street corners and speak about Christ," he said from his home in Don Mills, Ontario. "He was quite an eloquent preacher; his heart flamed as he gave out the message."

Railton got so caught up in his public preaching "that the boat upon which he was to have sailed left Halifax without him!"

Oops. A Sally Anne soldier stranded on the seashore! He missed the boat.

A Christian man named Saunders took the commissioner into his home. "Having a large parlor he invited some friends to come in for a meeting," said General Brown. This was the historic first meeting of the movement in our country.

Another gathering was held in a building on Argyle street which "at that time was being used as an art school."

After a quick check with the master of old city directories Terry Punch, I learned that the art school was likely in the building at the corner of Argyle and George streets—now the Five Fisherman restaurant and the so-called Liquor Dome of loud bars. The irony of this early Christian movement meeting in this den of liquidity I need not dwell on.

Railton's bombastic zeal mesmerized and inspired the public. "He was gregarious, outgoing, intellectual; a linguist," said General Brown.

Railton travelled the world, from Japan to China to Germany. But his independence caused friction with the founder of the fledgling Sally Anne movement, William Booth. "He [Railton] was a wandering kind of man," said Brown, "and sometimes he and William Booth disagreed on things because he was a…ahh…a *free character.*"

Oh, is that what they called it back then?

Railton signed an autograph book for the young girl in a home where he stayed. He left her a long enthusiastic, inspirational note often repeated by Army soldiers today.

In part, he wrote, "When saved, spend your life in saving others; the life of a soul saver is the grandest, merriest, strangest life that can be lived on earth."

Railton delivered the Salvation Army its first convert in Canada—a Haligonian man named Stoddard. But really the Sally Anne's invasion in Nova Scotia didn't officially happen until four years later.

It was amazing. It was August 9, 1885. Placards around the city announced the Army's arrival. Five thousand Haligonians came to watch the grand opening event. The *Halifax Herald* reported it was "one of the largest crowds ever congregated in this city on the Sabbath day."

They gathered on the Grand Parade, the downtown square, singing and marching. The crowds continued into the evening, called to services by the bells of St. Paul's church. The newspaper reported, "Brunswick and Prince streets, for a couple of blocks, were simply a sea of humanity."

After that, recruits started signing up and the Salvation Army movement marched along, expanding by year's end into New Glasgow, Truro, Dartmouth, and Stellarton.

Decades later, in the aftermath of the Halifax Explosion, the Salvation Army was very active in the relief effort. And of course they've stayed with us, offering their spiritual and social service where needed, as anyone born in their old Grace Maternity Hospital can attest. Just as Sally Anne was there for the birth of Grace babies, Halifax was there for Sally Anne's.

From Pictou to Panama

A globetrotting geologist solves
the great canal conundrum.

So, I've been digging into the Panama Canal. Yup. Got the scoop on all sorts of dirt. And rock. It seems this great waterway linking the world's two largest oceans was made possible in part by a genial genius geologist from Nova Scotia.

Dr. Donald F. MacDonald started life in 1875 in Egerton, Pictou County. A gentle giant sort, he laboured hard early in life but eventually became a man of science. By 1910, he was working for the United States Geological Survey when he was called to the Canal Zone. There was a major construction problem. Huge masses of rock were sliding down the muddy sides of the three-hundred-foot-wide gut as it was being cut. The rockslides were tremendous enough to form massive rock islands in the centre of the unfinished canal—a serious engineering setback.

Biographer Robert Legget says that D.F. MacDonald was the first to recognize the character of the deep-seated deformation of the rock. He studied the structure and the ground water around it. And he came up with a workable treatment for the builders' messy nemesis.

Bill Shaw, a geology teacher at Saint Francis Xavier University where Donald F. MacDonald also ended up teaching, explained to me that MacDonald was able to tell canal workers "which masses of rock were most likely to be involved in a slide." Preemptive geologizing!

The canal diggers were told to decrease the side slopes and dig straight down instead. That helped. And MacDonald also set up a monitoring system so engineers could detect small movements in the threatening rock. It was a piece of pioneering geology that added to MacDonald's growing international reputation. It allowed the famous canal to be completed.

This guy knew rocks and dirt real good.

He ought to have. He started out dirt poor. "Well he didn't have a lot," said Claire Grace, MacDonald's grand-niece in Antigonish. "He left home when he was pretty young. He travelled all of Canada before he was educated. He was only 16 or 17 when he left."

A quiet, mannered man—a field assistant claimed he saw MacDonald angry only once, when a wet stray dog crawled into his bedroll one night—MacDonald's physical look was not meek; he was a strong, square-jawed, keen-eyed, strapping Scot.

Before he started to dig rocks, MacDonald spent some rough years digging coal in mines, working on ships, labouring on the railroad and earning his living in a logging camp. He was with Hudson's Bay Company in Alaska. He organized a pack train into Dawson City at the time of the Klondike Gold rush.

Then this wilderness man came to academia. He knew he wanted to study the earth he had worked in, on, and under during his maturing years.

This rugged intellectual wound up in Seattle, Washington in full frontier garb (fur cap and moccasins) with four hundred bucks to his name. He began studying mining engineering at the University of Washington.

After specializing, MacDonald taught at American universities but he was a top-notch field geologist. Once, he found himself surrounded by blazing trees in an Idaho forest fire, barely escaping with his life. He worked for an oil

D.F. MacDonald, right, helped to save the Panama Canal, and Mrs. MacDonald, left.

company at one point and contracted tuberculosis in Albania. He recovered in Palermo, Italy. He also led an expedition for oil exploration in Costa Rica. All the while, he continued a consulting relationship with the famous canal, which needed ongoing maintenance.

In the 1930s, he settled back in Nova Scotia to teach geology at St.F.X.

But summer stints spent back in the Canal Zone led to a permanent placement there again once war broke out.

In 1939, MacDonald was called to become consulting geologist on the Canal's Third Locks Project. Though 64 years old, he responded out of duty.

He was needed to help widen the Panama Canal for new, larger ships of war. In a letter home to his St. F.X. University president, MacDonald wrote, "If I am needed here, I shall stick, bombs or no bombs. I feel that I best serve the great allied cause of freedom by working here as long as I may be needed."

A geologist hero!

MacDonald died while serving the war effort in his own way. He was buried in the Canal Zone after a solemn service attended by high level canal officials and the local governor. His wife, Lucy Hagan MacDonald, later had her husband's body reburied in her native Kentucky.

His was a full life worth digging into: Donald F. MacDonald, the Panamanian Pictonian!

Political Sidekick
to a Psychic

*The triumphant, tragic tale
of a possible prime minister.*

Pierre Trudeau, a passionate, patriotic prime minister, lay in state in our prestigious parliament buildings where long lines of mourners wound through echoing corridors to pay their respects. But the first to be so honoured in death was a politician from Nova Scotia who could have been prime minister. An advisor and close friend to eccentric Prime Minister Mackenzie King, Norman McLeod Rogers was a World War One veteran, a Rhodes scholar, university teacher and disciplined politician. A prime shaper of King's progressive social policies, he also tolerated the psychic spirituality of a political leader who saw dead people!

Born in Amherst in 1894, Rogers started his brilliant academic career at Acadia University, in Wolfville. Later he taught there. He also attended Oxford University, becoming political science chairman at Queen's in Kingston, Ontario. But he wasn't tied to academe's ivory tower. King made Rogers his private secretary in the 1920s.

The intellectual joined the blood sport of politics completely in 1935. Elected the federal Liberal member for Kingston, John A. Macdonald's old Tory riding, it was clear Mr. Rogers was brainy and gutsy.

He was an idealist, a reformer, an invaluable prodder and shaper of the government's social stance. Rogers' political star shone in Ottawa as minister of labour and then of defense.

According to King's diary, Rogers' personal relationship with the great prime minister also gleamed. Norman Hillman, a history teacher at Ottawa's Carleton University, told me King favoured this Nova Scotian as "a young man of principles, of ideas, of intellect."

Rogers and King were close. King thought Rogers had "a special quality about him," said Hillman, "and a special quality about his family." He "thought of him as Prime Ministerial timber."

Here's proof. It's a quote from PM King's diary, dated August 1936, as shared with me by Arthur Milnes of the Kingston *Whig-Standard*, "Rogers is the best all round man in the cabinet. He may yet be party leader and prime minister."

Even King's spirit-world side didn't come between King and his bond with this Nova Scotian. Once, the Prime Minister brought a psychic to Norman Rogers' house for a seance. The intellectual Rogers patiently participated then calmly said to his boss, "It's very nice but it isn't for me." Rogers was his own man.

His grandson, Halifax lawyer John MacLeod Rogers, is proud that, as federal minister of labour, Rogers brought in new unemployment insurance legislation. "He stopped the relief camps in the late 30s," said John Rogers as we talked in his harbourfront office.

As Canada's war-time defense minister, Norman Rogers "had been crucial in establishing the commonwealth air training plan—the foundation for training pilots all across the country for the allied war effort," said his grandson.

In the early war years, Norman Rogers met and worked with the likes of Winston Churchill, Neville Chamberlain, King George VI, and Franklin Roosevelt.

But his life was tragically cut short in June, 1940. Mackenzie King asked Rogers to fly from Ottawa to Toronto to deliver a crucial speech on the status of the allied war effort. The Royal Canadian Airforce bomber crashed into trees outside Toronto—all on board were killed in the flames. King was devastated. He had convinced the reluctant Rogers to make that flight to give that important speech.

Later, King held a seance with another psychic at which, he claimed, the deceased Norman Rogers appeared. Again, King's diary tells all: "She said, 'There is another person here of whom you were very fond....He tells me to tell you he is very well and very happy and working with you and others here.'"

"It was perfectly clear it was Norman Rogers," King wrote.

John Rogers is reminded of his grandfather's grandeur by a small scrap of the original, handwritten speech Rogers was to give before he was killed. The torn paper was found in the plane wreckage. It was "always at my grandmother's desk and then at my father's and now at my home," said John.

The words are inspiring for those fearful times: "In the faith we will fight on, we will endure and we will win!"

Initially interred with other veterans in Ottawa, Norman McLeod Rogers' remains were removed twenty years after his death. His widow, John Rogers' grandmother, brought his remains home to Nova Scotia where she had also returned to live.

This intellectual politician is buried with family in Willowbank Cemetery in Wolfville, the town where he began his remarkable career.

Oak Islanδ Enigma

The neverending story of the mysterious bottomless pit.

OK look, I'm only going to say this once. The Oak Island Story is not for me. Sure, just about everyone is fascinated by the strange tale of buried treasure. Not me. I just can't deal with it! It's a riddle wrapped in a mystery inside a deep hole. Over the last two centuries, many attempts to solve the long, vertical puzzle ended in failure or death. What is down that long treasure pit? Theories abound and intertwine. It's unfathomable. But for you, I dug into it.

Sure, there are plenty of popular books on this sexy subject. Selling stories of secret, buried coins is a quick way to unearth some coin for yourself. Here's the collective chronology of Oak Island theories and events I was able to draw from my varied reading. Check your local library for details.

The treasure hunt started in 1795 with a teenager named McGinnis. He was walking on the wooded island in beautiful Mahone Bay on Nova Scotia's south shore.

'X' didn't mark the spot. The ground was marked by a curious depression. (Haven't we all been, at times?) The teenager had heard tales of pirates in the area. So he and his friends dug. What they found astonished them. Two feet below the surface they came across a layer of flagstones covering the pit. At ten feet down they ran into a layer of oak logs spanning the pit. Again at twenty feet and thirty feet they found more log layers.

Years later, some diggers got down to ninety feet, finding a log layer at every ten foot interval. As well, at forty feet, a layer of charcoal was found; at fifty feet, a layer of putty. And 60 feet down, a layer of coconut fibre. That's right, coconut fibre. I am not making this up. This strange layering of materials continued. The pit seemed endless.

An 1849 group with a drill brought up a revealing core sample. At 98 feet the drill went through a spruce platform. Then it encountered 4 inches of oak and then 22 inches of what was characterized as "metal in pieces." Next, 8 inches of oak, another 22 inches of metal, 4 inches of oak and another layer of spruce. The conclusion was that they had drilled through 2 casks or chests filled with coins!

Oak Island: so simple from above, so complex underneath!

More mystery: a rock slab etched with an odd coded message was found ninety feet down. In 1866, a Halifax language specialist transcribed it this way, "Forty feet below two million pounds are buried." But like almost everything in this saga, that's been contested.

More core samples showed evidence of a concrete vault, deep down. But that's contested too. Also, bits of old lettered parchment turned up on the drill blades. It's all very curious.

Booby trapped as it is with flood tunnels and a decoy treasure, this odd hole in the earth must be hiding something valuable.

What's really down there? Ready for the theories? They run the gamut from the Holy Grail itself to Captain Kidd's treasure to Shakespeare's original works. You see why I didn't want to touch this one?

One Oak Island researcher suggests that the poet Sir Francis Bacon was the true author of things Shakespearean and he felt his original manuscripts so vital to man that they required special preservation. Since he was a friend of fellow Mason William Alexander, the founder of New Scotland, Sir Bacon picked Oak Island as the time capsule for his lofty writings. So the theory goes.

Maybe. Could be.

Followers of Prince Henry Sinclair believe the Scottish Prince sailed here before Columbus. As the keeper of the legendary Holy Grail, preserved by an ancient order called the Knights of Malta, Prince Henry needed a safe place for the ancient cup.

Oak Island? Sure. Why not?

Perhaps Shakespeare's complete works and Christ's holy chalice were flown to Mahone Bay by green aliens, avowing Christianity and spouting Hamlet!

Yeah, that's it! It could happen.

As for it being Captain Kidd's treasure buried on the island, well, that's just not farfetched enough to be believed now is it?

Maybe a psychic would help. Nope. One treasure hunter even tried that and got nowhere.

Read the books. It seems everything's been tried.

In the 1970s, new technology came to the island. A camera lowered down to a bedrock cavity at 230 feet returned amazing images: a severed hand floating in the water, three chests (of the treasure type I would presume), various tools and, finally, a human body. More death. Yet modern-day treasure hunters keep trying.

Expensive attempts to solve the Oak Island puzzle continue. No luck yet.

So, let's see. Two centuries. Millions spent. Lives lost. Lots of wacky theories. And still no workable way to reach the alleged treasure. It seems it's a tale with no end about a pit with no bottom!

A Woman's Work
Is with a Gun

*Our first female woods guide remembers
old Nova Scotia.*

A woman's work is never done—in the woods. That was mostly true in this thickly-treed province during the early half of the 1900s. But one woodsy woman stood out from the crowd. You might say she could see the forest *and* the trees.

Her name now is Molly Wilson. But she was born Molly Hunt—an appropriate name because years ago she was quite a crack shot with a rifle. In an interview with the local paper, *The Coastguard*, Molly said she shot animals for food when she was ten years old living in Queens County, on the South Shore.

Those were Molly's 'Davey Crockett' days. Or should I say, 'Daisy Crockett.'

Molly became a licensed woods guide—likely the first female in Nova Scotia to do so. Her father ran her grandfather's resort, the Maple Leaf Hotel in Greensfield, near Liverpool, Queen's County. Molly remembers when British and American sportsmen came there to fish thirty-pound salmon and to hunt moose. They needed guides for hunting and fishing so Molly learned the art of guiding from her three brothers. She took to paddling birchbark canoes, shooting game, and sleeping outside on beds of spruce bows. She wore soft moccasins for stealth in the woods. Her brothers will tell you Molly was quite adept in the wilds.

And yet Molly modestly claims, with a chuckle, that she didn't do the kind of guiding the men did.

"I would take perhaps a woman in a canoe for some fishing," she told me, "while her husband was going down the river with a 'real' guide."

So it's only real guiding if your client is male? I don't buy it. To me, Molly seemed as woods-aware as a guide needed to be. She talked about canoeing up the grand Mersey River and paddling into the untouched Tobiatic wilderness, near Kejimkujik National Park.

Those places are isolated enough today; imagine what they were like in the 1920s and 30s! Longfellow had it right; Nova Scotia *was* "the forest primeval." I know *I* couldn't do it.

Molly also did her share of 'women's' work. She helped out around the family's hotel doing housecleaning chores. At times her family followed her father deeper into the woods where he worked in a lumber camp. "We stayed in camps when we were children in the winter. Mother would prepare our lessons and we'd come back to school in the spring," she said.

During World War One, Molly's father, 'Link' Hunt, was in France—in charge of a lumbering operation, supplying planks for Allied troops in the trenches. Until his return, her mother had to run the business and raise the children alone. Quite a female role model for rugged young Molly! The forest taught Molly its own lessons.

"It was the primitive life of Nova Scotia in those days," she said, "and from that I probably developed self reliance and love of nature."

By age 19 Molly found she was a big hit at a Boston sportsman's show, marching behind the Royal Canadian Highland Band in her leather moccasins and her brown woodsman's clothes. She was a good shot with a hand gun and rifle. Shooting was second nature to her, but Molly knows that being female put her on the front page of the *Boston Globe*.

"I wasn't unattractive and to have a girl was a novelty," she said. "It appealed to the reporters and they featured me more than I deserved."

The media-savvy Molly laughed in retrospect: "It's kind of silly now."

As a young woman, Molly lived in Boston a while, became a book-keeper briefly in Halifax, eloped to Maine and later lived a married life in Ontario. Widowed, Molly retired to Rockland, Shelburne County where she remarried, taking the name Wilson.

When Molly and I chatted, she was a brand new ninety year old. She had long since given up hunting—for hooking. From being a rifle shooter, she became a rug hooker.

I can't do *that* either!

The Lie Detector: a Nova Scotian Invention

Maybe it is, maybe it isn't.

The truth shall set you free! Nova Scotians have long loved a good fish or folk tale but we know a fib when we hear it. Would you believe the lie detecting machine was created by a Bluenose inventor?

Well, actually he 'helped develop' the lie detector. Truth be told, no single inventor gets the credit—the science of lie detecting evolved gradually. But it was mightily advanced in the 1920s by a talented psychiatrist from Nova Scotia: Dr. John Augustus Larson, born in Shelburne on December 11, 1892.

The polygraph machine *per se* began to take shape during Dr. Larson's lifetime. American specialist Bill Marston was testing 'deception tests' for possible use in World War One counter-intelligence.

A fledgling psychologist at the time, Dr. Larson grew intrigued and added his own contributions to fib finding. He is known for making the machine portable by attaching the various testing devices (respiration, heart rate, and blood pressure monitors) to one flat piece of wood. It became known as Larson's 'bread board polygraph.' The board made the equipment moveable and practical for police work.

His lie detector equipment boasted several other major improvements over other designs. First, it brought together several devices to be used at the same time. He amalgamated the many to a single unit; hence this Nova Scotian put the 'poly' in the 'polygraph.'

Also, Larson's truth-testing measurements weren't as intermittent as they were on some other machines. His bread board instruments continually and simultaneously measured respiration and cardiovascular changes in the test subject.

All that lie detector stuff you see in the TV cop shows—it was his idea. Including a brilliant little gizmo called the event marker. The little doo-hickey marked the machine's paper read-out, showing when the subject's verbal response to a question began and when it ended. That's important. Checking the zig zag line on the paper read-out, the tester could look for changes in the subject's bodily responses that occurred while the subject was answering specific questions. The moments of higher stress could be pinpointed. And therein lies the lie. Ingenious!

Larson even developed the control-question technique, honing the kind of questions asked in the tests. ("Did you do it?" would have been a good one, I'm guessing.)

A pioneer of lie detection technology, his modifications advanced the science substantially.

Don't take my word for it. I learned all this from a lie detector expert who is often called to testify in court about the validity of today's deception detectors. Dr. James Matte in New York is the author of an eight-hundred-page book called *Forensic Psychophysiology Using the Polygraph*. (If a judge ever threatens to "throw the book at you," you'd better hope it isn't this one.)

Dr. Matte told me in a telephone interview that a murder and a college girl's underwear were the focus of two separate crimes that Larson's machine helped solve in the 1920s. In the first case, he found the missing body. In the other, he found the miss's bodice.

"Ninety college girls, in a college boarding house," said Dr. Matte, "had been victimized by a series of larcenies including: silk underwear, a registered letter, and a diamond ring. All the girls were tested, with their consent, using a cardio-neural psychograph (an early lie detector). The recording showed a marked uniformity for all the girls with one exception."

That one exception was the guilty girl. She confessed and returned the items, including the silky unmentionables. You see, a good lie detector can uncover the most intimate secret. Even Victoria's Secret.

This Bluenose boy abroad lived a full life of lies. As an eminent psychiatrist, Dr. Larson taught physiology at the University of California, Berkeley. He used his lie detector in work for the Berkeley police. He also lectured in forensic psychiatry for the Honolulu police department. He worked all over the United States in psychiatry, neuropsychiatry, criminology and shock therapy. He studied fingerprinting, tattoo symbolization, and psychobiology. He's listed in *Who Was Who* in America.

Larson's father, John Senior, was born in Sweden. His mother, Lucina Mack, was from Mill Village, near Liverpool. The Shelburne County Genealogical Society confirmed, without word of a lie, Larson's Shelburne birth. And that's the truth. Honest.

Dartmouth's Mystery House, Then and Now

The history of the mystery and modern-day hauntings too.

The doctor vanished without a trace. One hundred and fifty-five years later, the house where he stayed on the hill overlooking the harbour is still known as the "Mystery House" of Dartmouth. Dr. John McDonald, originally from Irvin, Invernesshire, Scotland, was a well-respected family physician. He was a Justice of the Peace, governor on the board of Dalhousie College and an eligible bachelor. But in 1846, he disappeared amid controversy and confusion.

Dr. McDonald boarded at the respectable rooming house at 95 King Street, on Blockhouse Hill, old Dartmouth's highest land mass (across from the fire station).

When I visited the house, Dr. Dan Bunbury, a historian renting the large home, greeted me with his own research into Mystery House lore. A James Thorpe ran it as a boarding house in the 1840s. Thorpe claimed that Dr. McDonald seemed absentminded and looked unsettled at the time he vanished. But others reported no change in the doc's demeanor that week.

"Supposedly," said Dr. Bunbury, "he got up, said 'see you later' to his fellow boarders, left the house and was perfectly fine. So that was the mystery. Was he indeed upset or not? No one really knew for sure."

Why slip away? Here are a few clues to the mystery.

Dartmouth historian John Martin wrote that Dr. McDonald had a half brother, Allen McDonald, a well-off Dartmouth merchant who ran the Way Office, an early post office on Portland Street near the ferry terminal. According to Martin, the doctor wanted to give up his practice. He purchased a third of Allen's business and became a partner. Why give up medicine for merchandising? That's a mystery in itself. Later there were rumours of embezzlement. Court documents show that after Allen died, Dr. McDonald acted oddly in running the store, occasionally closing it down during usually busy business days.

Then, one day, he was gone!

Rumours spread. Speculation abounded. Townsfolk began a hunt for the missing man. Some claimed they saw him on the Halifax side waiting for a boat. Others said they saw him leave the Dartmouth post office without his trademark walking stick and spectacles. The *Halifax Times* reported the doctor was spotted in St. John, New Brunswick. The copper mine in Dartmouth was drained of water in search of the lost doc's body. No luck. He simply vanished. Or maybe not so simply.

Stories had developed of a secret underground tunnel from the Mystery House down to the harbour waters, the doctor's escape route perhaps. Dan invited me in to investigate.

At the end of the hardwood floor in the ground level family room, a short door opened to a compact, brick chamber, a tiny wine cellar, with a low vaulted ceiling. Dan pointed to a brick wall that had been smashed through, showing another brick wall behind it. What's behind wall number two? "You can only imagine where that would go," said Dan. Was he serious or mocking?

After all, Dartmouth's early settlement was protected by a square wooden fortification, a blockhouse, which folklore alleges had a tunnel running from it to the water. The blockhouse would have been just across the street from the Mystery House. Perhaps the disappearing doc decided to dash with stolen cash via the soldiers' secret passage to the shore.

The Ph.D in history beside me smiled. Sure, a tunnel was possible but "you'd only have about half a mile of solid rock to get through," he said flatly. Darn realist!

Sensing my disappointment, Dan piped up with news of a buried skull beneath the floorboards of the Mystery House. Great! More mystery. The skull had turned up in 1879, about thirty years after the doc's disappearance. Speculation ran wild. Was this all that remained of Dr. John McDonald?

An inquest was held. Another doctor, D.W. Weeks, examined the skull and he recognized it. It was the skull of one of the poor mutinous sailors of the ill-fated vessel *Saladin*. The hanging of those sailors was a major public spectacle in Halifax in 1844.

Dartmouth's Mystery House: three storeys, woodstove, haunted. Possible secret tunnel.

The infamous souvenir skull had passed through many hands until a woman in the mystery house took possession. She wanted rid of it, so buried it where no one would see her disposing of it.

"She simply hid it in the mystery house below the floor," Dan explained.

So that's Dartmouth's Mystery House, site of an unusual disappearance and an unexpected discovery. But more modern mysteries continue to haunt the house on the hill.

On my next visit to the house, two years later, its new owner was living there. I met with Paul McVicar, a structural inspector with the navy, and his friend Maureen King, a physiotherapist. We had invited along a previous owner who had lived there 25 years earlier, Rosemary Beckett, a civil servant. All three reported unnatural occurrences and strange sensations within that old house.

Paul said he saw a doorknob turning on its own. Rosemary claimed, when she lived there in the 1970s, a fully-uniformed seventeenth-century soldier appeared briefly downstairs. Maureen and Paul both spent a frightful, sleepless night in the fall of 2000, agitated by repeated noises coming from the main floor. First it was a pile of metal rods in the workshop area that suddenly spilled off a shelf to the concrete floor breaking the stillness of the night., then it was the roar of a fire in the woodstove that previously had been down to just embers. When Paul went down to investigate, lifting the round black metal cover off the stove with its handle, the heavy iron disk flew up in the air, clattering to the floor beside him. He was spooked. Maureen vowed never to spend that night of the year in that house again.

It was November 30, the anniversary of Dr. MacDonald's mysterious disappearance 155 years earlier.

Bug Beater

The itches to riches story of the inventor of Muskol.

O ur searing summer sun can leave plants parched. Our thick winter snows can weigh heavily on hibernating horticulture. Growing stuff can be challenging here. But there's one robust crop Nova Scotia never struggles to produce: interesting characters. I mean the unusual, creative, sometimes goofy, often brilliant, differently-thinking, marching-to-an-ad-lib-beat type of people—characters! We enjoy a healthy harvest of them and we're all the healthier for them. Heck, some weeks I live off 'em!

Imagine a Nova Scotian man in a big Stetson, a long waxed-to-a-point mustache, spectacles, grey beard, and moose hide jacket. He might strike you as Colonel Sanders on safari. Now picture Col. Sanders on safari in a fire-engine-red Mercedes station

Recognize this Muskol man? Nova Scotia's Charlie Coll.

wagon, cruising the streets of Truro. Oh yeah, he also sported a necklace of gold mosquitoes around his neck. Now, THAT'S an interesting character.

His off-beat appearance betrayed his off-the-beaten-track view of life. A clever inventor and salesman, he brought his novel product to a level of international recognition and made himself a big name and a huge bank account. And it all came from a popular bug spray. This character was Charlie Coll—or Col. Coll—the brain behind the popular insect repellent Muskol.

Charlie Coll's musky liquid, nemesis to black flies and mosquitoes, was featured in magazines and on T.V. consumer shows. Muskol became known as the best bug beater for woodsman or weekend camper. The label reads, "Proudly Canadian since 1951." Charlie made big bucks from little bugs. It's weird to think his insect empire started in his humble basement in New Glasgow. No, it's really not weird. Sounds like the start of any great invention doesn't it? A germ of an idea, a wild thought, a casual first attempt, local interest, news spreads, the basement becomes too small, soon millions from international marketing begin pouring in. I've seen it before. It seems to happen to those differently-wired individuals in Nova Scotia like Charlie Coll, the Fuller Brush Man, and Alex G. Bell. Never to me for some reason.

Born in Stewiacke, Coll followed his father's footsteps into the hard-rock mining life of northern Quebec. He literally broke his back doing that work. Coll then returned to his home province, to live in Pictou County near his mother's people, the Sutherlands. It was the place of his roots. His father had helped sink the Allen shaft in Stellarton after a mine explosion near the turn of the century.

In New Glasgow, Charlie worked for Tibbet paint.

Apparently unafraid to try anything once, he took over the paint lab when the chemist left. Why not? Charlie had been a chem lab assistant for one summer, thirty years earlier. Perfectly qualified to make tough Tibbet paint. Well, he muddled through.

He wasn't really the laboratory type. He was the outdoorsy, Hemingway type. One day he read an article about the American military's use of a strong liquid chemical on soldiers serving in jungles.

Diethyl-M-Toluomide was the stuff, a corrosive chemical known as DEET. The military was using it full-strength, which sounds risky. But then, they also dabbed agent orange behind their ears. Nevertheless, they used pure DEET and Charlie was intrigued. He ordered a small batch from the company man who happened to visit the paint plant. Pouring some DEET in small drugstore bottles in his basement, Charlie made it available to the public, full-strength.

Hunters learned the musky scent covered up their own and it also attracted their prey. The deer liked DEET. But the bugs were bugged. To them DEET was death. Or at least a bad stink. Mosquitoes kept their distance. But not the poor hunter's wife, laundering the DEET-soaked clothes. She couldn't avoid the smell. Many will forever have the pungent scent in their nostrils.

Charlie's move to Truro brought his production plant out of the cellar into the garage. His first wholesale gallon of DEET became five gallons, then a tanker truck full. *Sports Afield* magazine got wind of the musky scent and wrote about it. The publicity quickly helped turn Charlie's garage plant into a repel-lent bottling factory with twenty employees. Charlie's new venture was taking off. You might say, he had worked out all the bugs.

The two-syllable product name came from the deermusk smell of the liquid, and Charlie's last name, Coll, which rhymes with 'call.' Hence, Muskol, guaranteed to give you 'bug-off' protection for eight hours.

A Canadian and American patent guaranteed Charlie years of protection from the bite of commercial predators.

Charlie's patented Muskol was 95 percent DEET and 5 percent 'related toluomides.' Pungent and powerful.

In 1978, the CBC Television program "Marketplace" sniffed around Charlie's burgeoning bug business. Known for their tough-minded consumer journalism and relatively attractive anchor folk, the coverage boosted Charlie's sales again.

The media-wise salesman knew how to give a good clip.

"Fourteen women," said Charlie to the T.V. camera, "went on a jungle safari in a swamp in Colombia and they took 6 dozen of my stuff back there and I got pictures from England of the women with short sleeves and low necks in the jungle in South America!"

"It gives me quite a kick," he said.

It seems Charlie's musky product packed quite a kick too. Chuck Coll, Charlie Coll junior, living in Pictou County, helped his father build his Muskol business. He told me the high concentration of DEET did much more than repel bugs.

Apparently Charlie senior's Muskol also had a corrosive quality to watch out for. That part astonished me. But Chuck didn't seem fazed when we talked. Here's our conversation:

"At that time it was the only product that worked," said Chuck. "It was good for eight hours. The only thing that was negative about it," he said, "was that you had to wash your hands after you put it on, or it would do damage to plastic and steering wheels and golf clubs and things like that."

Excuse me? He didn't seem to see anything wrong with what he said but I was baffled. Questioning further didn't seem to help.

Me: "It would eat through plastic?"

Him: "Oh yeah, it was great."

Me: "People were rubbing this on their skin though?"

Him: "Oh yeah."

Me: "That wasn't a problem?"

Him: "No."

Me: "It wouldn't eat through skin?"

Him: "No."

Me: "Just plastic?"

Him: "Yup."

Me: "Ooookay."

How curious and bizarre. Why this pungent potion repelled bugs, melted plastic, and didn't hurt human skin was beyond me. That's what puts the 'mystery' in 'chemistry' I guess. Parents have smeared this odorous stuff on their kids for decades. As far as I know, none has yet disintegrated.

According to the inventor's son, as long as you didn't spill the bottle in your knapsack and melt your Swiss Army knife, Muskol would keep the bugs at bay for a day, no problem. It passed all the food and drug regulations and remains on the market.

Huge conglomerates like Johnson and Johnson liked what they heard. They began circling and moving in to draw blood. Charlie's patent restricted them from selling the high levels of undiluted DEET that Charlie was selling: 95 percent proof. They turned on the competitive heat: Their bug products versus Charlie's. Price wars were imminent. But the Colls were into heavy production.

"By this time about 85 percent of the sales were in the States," said Chuck Coll.

"We were bringing the DEET up in tanker truck loads from North Carolina and bottling it and sending it back!"

Muskol was being sent to Australia, parts of Africa, and Europe as well. As the small bottles were drained, the money poured in. As the money poured in, Charlie Coll danced out. Whenever he could, he was off playing the Hemingway from Nova Scotia, hunting and fishing in exotic places, travelling the world, pursuing his outdoorsman passions. He wore his string of gold mosquitoes around his neck with mirthful glee; a triumph and a tribute. He beat the bug and it made him a fortune.

Eventually, the patent on Muskol ran out. The buzzing predators began pushing copycat products. Chuck Coll told me Deep Woods Off was created to take on Muskol in the market. Charlie agreed with his son, it was a good time to sell out. He died in 1981. Not long after, the business was sold.

Today, Charlie's musky Muskol carries on his legacy. The new owner still sells the yellowish oil under the same name. And each little bottle still carries Charlie Coll's characteristically smiling portrait with the big Stetson, flamboyant mustache, grey beard, and moose hide coat.

What a character.

The Longest Serving Santa

A lifetime of Christmas spirit
in a Digby County village.

On a snowy Christmas morning in 1912, in a tiny Digby County village, a Christmas miracle occurred. Willis Tibbetts, an energetic farmer, lumberman, and handyman, was up early that bright holy day morning, shovelling the Christmas Eve snow from his walk. Taken by the spirit of the season, he was moved to also clear his next-door neighbour's walk. The neighbour's children awoke later and immediately thought the snowy path out front had been magically created by Santa Claus!

Their innocent imaginations touched Willis and transformed his life forever. He decided then and there he would become Father Christmas for all the children of the twin villages of Brighton and Barton, near the head of St. Mary's Bay. And that he did, every Christmas Eve for sixty years! Right up into his nineties! Old Santa himself would be impressed.

Life had never been easy for Willis. Born into rural poverty in 1881, Willis' mother died when he was a baby. Another family raised him. With little education, he worked his way to New England, eventually becoming a faithful officer in the Salvation Army. He returned to Nova Scotia to work the land and care for an injured brother. He went to school as an adult, learned to read, and began a life of service to local children. A committed Salvationist, Willis married a Sally Anne officer in Digby who was claimed by illness within a few years. He was left with no mother for his children, yet he kept on giving to his community. Willis served as YPSM, the Young People's Sergeant Major. He treated kids to picnics on his land in summer. But each December 24, his mission was to do Santa's work.

The white beard was a given. At first it was a simple stringy thing. He fashioned a belt of bells to strap round his pillowed belly, cinching his red Santa suit tight. A wiry, muscled labourer, he wasn't quite the right build. But anyway, his heart was in it. Oh boy, was it ever.

Sure, he did the usual Christmas concert appearances for the Sally Anne and other denominations. Even into his 50s, this jolly fit elf would appear suited on stage doing a summersault to the children's delight. Into his eighties he would ride his bike the seven miles into Digby. But Willis Tibbetts' Christmas Eve home visits were the most special.

There's a Santa in every mall these days. But back then, back there, a Santa at your door brought your young imagination to life!

Nola Jeffrey remembers the magic. In 1940 she was a young believer. Her Christmas memories of those magical moments in tiny Brighton are still brushed in her mind like an impressionist painting—fuzzy edged, but brilliantly bright in spots. The images of Santa swirl with the joy, the sounds, the smells of her childhood Christmas.

Nola is a retired teacher who hasn't lived in Brighton in decades. But she pulled back the curtain of time on her old painting of memories and let me peek into the past.

Imagine: It's Christmas Eve and five-year-old Nola is excited. She's been waiting all evening, and her mother has fresh-baked cookies cooling. Oh, the sound of jingling bells outside! A knock at the kitchen door! It blows open to a blustery whoosh of snow, and there he is! A tall, jolly, white-bearded Santa in his red suit. The bells are jingling. He's ho-ho-hoing.

Willis Tibbetts in an early Santa suit: bringing joy door to door for over 50 years.

And young Nola's eyes are wide in amazement. Santa is in her kitchen!

"You would almost expect he had the reindeer waiting right outside," she told me.

Each Christmas Eve, Willis Tibbetts visited every child's house in the Brighton/Barton area. "He would laugh and talk and give us candy," said Nola.

Sometimes he gave small toys contributed by local folk. Then he'd move on. He covered about fifty houses in one evening. He did that every year for six decades, from 1912 up to 1972, stopping only a few years before he passed away at age 94. If you ask me, Willis *was* Santa Claus. He captured the spirit.

Generations of Brighton and Barton children knew Willis Tibbetts as "Santa Claus." That's who he was to them. His son Francis, now living in Eastern Passage, is happy to let his father's Santa story be told. It's a unique record: the longest serving Sally Anne Santa, perhaps anywhere.

Francis keeps his Dad's memory alive by keeping some old photos of his father as Father Christmas. That's not all he keeps. As we spoke he gave his father's old Santa bells a shake on their worn leather harness. The nostalgic jingle-jingle of the bells had an instant emotional effect. Such a sweet, sweet sound. I imagined I was five and I shivered.

Merry Christmas.

A League of Her Own

A female first steps up to bat in New York City.

If you are a faithful fan of the great game who wants to worship at baseball's hallowed Hall of Fame, your pilgrimage should take you to Cooperstown, New York. Nova Scotia has its own Hall of Fame with its own unique road into baseball history, a road that also takes you to New York—to New York City, where our first professional female athlete played for an all-female ball team.

Really!

Sixty-six years ago, Edna Lockhart Duncanson was magically

propelled into the final perfect year of a baseball team that changed her life forever. She owes it all to a Baptist minister with good sporting contacts.

It was 1935. The 17-year-old from Avonport, Kings County was in New York visiting her sister. When the minister came by, Edna was out on the street where two New York gals were tossing a ball. She joined in. The minister came out after a while, watched the game of catch, then walked over to speak to Edna.

"I know a lady who owns a baseball team," he said.

Edna—now in her 80s—was describing that chance meeting to me like it was yesterday. The minister knew Margaret Nable, apparently one of the better female coaches in America at the time.

"He said, 'do you mind if I give her your name,'" Edna told me.

By the next day, after one rehearsal, she was pitching in her first professional game, with the New York Bloomer Girls. I guess if men's teams can be named after red or white socks, why not a young women's team named after underwear?

Edna came by it naturally. Growing up in Avonport, she played all sorts of sports: basketball, tennis, softball. She was a swimmer too.

She even laced up the skates to play hockey. She laced on the gloves to try boxing. A brotherly nose-bloodying or two didn't keep her from pursuing the sweet smell of victory. She rarely won a boxing bout with the boys but baseball, that was another thing.

The Bloomer Girls played everywhere. About a hundred games a year. Against men! That's right, Edna doesn't recall playing any female teams. In their white uniforms with the black stripes, the Bloomer Girls strutted their athletic stuff all over the American States.

"New York, Pennsylvania, Massachusetts, New Hampshire, Maryland, Delaware, right down to the Carolinas, the Virginias and beyond," she said.

The Bloomer girls travelled in two open cars that season of '35. They'd sack out in motels and farmhouses, changing from their skirts into uniforms before a game. They would play, win, then drive another hundred miles to play again, sometimes on the same day.

"We had no extras," she said. "We had a great time. It was a great learning experience for me; tremendous."

According to Edna, the New York Bloomer Girls were undefeated over their 25 year life span. Edna helped maintain that perfect record in that last glorious season. She was a pitcher who had to throw hard against the men at bat. She also played third base at times. That's where, she recalls, a runner plowed through her, planting Edna on her face. But she still came up with the ball! The depression era crowd cheered! They loved the games. It was good, rugged fun in a bad, rugged time.

Bloomer Girl baseball was grand entertainment, especially the day Edna "lambasted one over right field; a home run right in the thistles and bushes and thorns."

Ouch!

"They couldn't get it out. That's how I got a home run," she said, still chuckling with pride after all those years.

Edna recalls taking on The House of David, a men's team of former major leaguers and young players starting their careers. What a great game that must have been.

This athletic girl from rural Nova Scotia loved the big city of New York. Even after the team came to an end and the bloom was off the Bloomers, Edna decided she'd return to New York in 1936. She landed a job in a department store while also playing softball and, later, semi-pro basketball with the Staten Island Shamrocks.

Edna Lockhart Duncanson; baseball diamonds were this girl's best friend!

She liked the taste of the Big Apple.

But she liked the Annapolis Valley apples more, it seemed. Edna came home to Nova Scotia. She settled with her husband in Gaspereau, Kings County, she took a business course and exercised her singing voice. Now 80-something, Edna is still an outstanding athlete! When we talked, she had a bowling score of 307.

Yet baseball is still in her blood. She watches today's major leaguers running about her TV screen. She jolts and jeers and moves with their moves. An ardent armchair athlete, she forgets her age when the game's in full swing. When the anthem is sung and the players hit the field and the crowd roars for their favorites, it's as if she's on the field with them, in her black and white uniform, throwing the ball, swinging the bat, racing the bases and cheering her team…at the old ball game.

Street Lights and Spruce Trees

The amazing electric city in Nova Scotia's woods.

S hiny electric street lights in the middle of the dark Digby County woods over a hundred years ago—I was skeptical at first that this place existed. But it's true. It was New France, founded in 1895. Like some sort of magical fairy village, it was hidden about a full day's ox cart ride from Weymouth into the deep turn-of-the-century woods. This bustling brightly lit oasis in the dark forest was owned by one family.

Its founder, Emile Stehelin from Alsace, left his French homeland to create this little New France in Nova Scotia. It was hundreds of acres along the Silver River, near Langford Lake. Emile Stehelin's residence, the Big House, sat by a sort of town square surrounded by a forge, chapel, office building, club house, cook house, dog kennels, huge barn, and a water-powered saw mill, all circled by train tracks made out of round logs. It was a pole railway, made from skinned maple trees laid end to end.

Stehelin and his wife Anne had eight sons and four daughters. They ran the large family lumber business which employed many hardworking Nova Scotian lumbermen. This amazing place of industry in the middle of nowhere was known as the Electric City.

Paul Stehelin, the great grandson of the village founder, remembers from his great uncles' stories that the sawmill had a large generator powered by the river current.

"All of the buildings had electric lights in them," he said, "and there were street lights on the square and so the whole village was electrified."

It shone in isolation like a magical Santa's village, bustling with workers. Electric power was new to the province. It certainly hadn't reached remote rural areas.

Emile Stehelin came here with his family when he was 59 years old. He was a successful factory owner and locomotive builder. But he found the business atmosphere at home in Alsace too restricted after the political fallout from the Franco-Prussian war. He grew interested in this new world through a priest friend associated with College Sainte Anne in Digby County.

New France: an electrified village deep in the woods of old Nova Scotia.

The Stehelins made a good but unusual impression on local Weymouth folk. They were French but not Acadian. They wore unusual leather boots and drank imported wine as they entertained guests at their woodsy estate.

Emile, I am told, had a bold philosophy about worker freedoms. He didn't believe in authoritarian control over the working class. To free them from dependence on his company store, he paid cash for his men's labour so that —unlike the coalminer's 'pluck-me' stores of the time—the lumbermen could choose where to get their goods.

New France even boasted ethnic diversity in its labouring lumbermen. Paul Stehelin told me the workers included "the Mi'kmaq, the Acadians, the Anglos from Weymouth and the Blacks who came up and settled after the civil war."

This harmony of cultures thrived a century ago. "Maybe you can do that in the middle of the woods," Paul mused.

The inhabitants of New France eventually left their electric Eden. Anne, the matriarch of the Stehelin family, died in 1912. Her husband, Emile, unable to live without her in the lighted village he founded, moved into Weymouth. The Electric City dimmed.

The Stehelin sons moved on to other things, some to war. The daughters left too. The village in the woods was empty, a paradise lost.

Not long after, the founder's favorite horse, named General, as if sensing the end of an era, also disappeared from his new Weymouth home one day. The founder sent people to search. They went as far as the old village in the woods.

"They came to the square in New France and of course no one was there, it was deserted," said Paul, "and General was there, dead. That was the end of that saga."

Emile Stehelin died in Weymouth in 1918.

And yet the light of the old Electric City still softly shines in Paul Stehelin's warm descriptions of his family's homestead. Though he lives out of province, he keeps a cabin in the old New France woodland. He still goes back there to fish and hunt and have a drink with older local folk, swapping stories about what used to be and how marvelous it was.

"It's a link with the past, a link with the people," said Paul. "To me it's continuity."

Ríg Rescue!

*A gutsy sailor saves four from
an oil rig in a hurricane.*

T he giant jack-up oil rig Offshore 55 was in danger. Being towed by a tug from Trinidad to Texas, through the Caribbean Sea to the Gulf of Mexico, the crew was headed straight into the worst hurricane in twenty years. It was October 1961.

The tug crew knew they couldn't outrun the killer storm while towing a monstrous oil rig on a wire cable. But there were four engineers on the rig so they couldn't just cut it adrift. The tug captain had stupidly delayed removing them. Now it was too risky to manoeuvre that close. The giant swells of Hurricane Hattie were upon them.

John Moffat, the tugboat's second engineer, remembers those wild conditions. Now retired from sea life in Chilliwack, British Columbia, he told me by phone that the waves that day were "mountainous; in the 40-60 foot range!"

The massive oil rig bobbed like a tub toy.

"The forward corner of the rig would be 3 or 4 feet under water," said John, "and then the next minute it would be about 15 -20 feet above the water!"

To further the crisis, a wave smashed one of the men against metal machinery and his leg shattered. Two of them couldn't even swim, and all were nearly frozen with fear.

Enter the real-life hero: The first officer of the tugboat—The

Reg Caldwell rescues men from drifting oil rig in hurricane seas: heroic courage.

Sudbury Two—was the late Reg Caldwell, Halifax-born, living in Chester, Lunenburg County at the time. John Moffat is still in awe of what his Nova Scotian shipmate did that day.

Reg Caldwell took charge. He told the ineffective captain to sail within two hundred feet of the heaving oil rig. Since the tugboat's winch was broken, they cut the tow cable away.

"By using a special rocket gun," said John, "Reg fired a

line across the gap, which snared onto the handrails of the oil rig barge."

The men on the rig tied the rope to the rig's railing.

Then, Reg tied his end of the line to what's called a Carley float—a rigid floatation device, a rubber dinghy with a floor of canvas slats used in rescues. He climbed in the float. With the oil rig men pulling the line, and the tugboat men letting out another rope line, Reg's float was manoeuvred toward the men on the oil rig as it heaved high and fell fast. "Often Reg was looking down at them and other times he was looking up at them," said John.

The panicky injured man was first off.

"Reg managed to talk him into scrambling through the railing around the rig and waiting there with his lifejacket on and when a high enough wave came along, to just let go and let the wave carry him off the rig," said John.

"Reg then came into his own and swam after him and picked him up and got him onto the raft." He floated with the injured man back to the tug, then returned to the rig, riding the rollercoaster waves to save the others. The other nonswimmer was shuttled over. Then, the other two rode the rescue float to the tug, one at a time. In the end, Reg was left standing on the rig, last to leave. All this took about two hours.

Reg later described the rescue to his old sailing buddy George Lutz in Halifax. George brought Reg's story to me, describing proudly how Reg would have to get to the rig "just as the deck of the rig was level with the wave, otherwise he would have been crushed!"

"The end result was: he saved the lives of four men," said George. The tug speeded safely from the path of the approaching hurricane. The injured man was treated and picked up by the U.S. Navy. The rig drifted three hundred miles and was eventually found beached at British Honduras, embedded in a coral reef. It took six weeks for a salvage crew to free it. And the same tug, the Sudbury Two, retrieved it and delivered it to a port in Texas.

What kind of a man risks such a rescue?

Those who knew him say Reg Caldwell had a commanding demeanor about him. He was a voracious reader of technical manuals and taught John Moffat how to navigate by the stars. A war veteran, he served as a propeller mechanic with the Royal Canadian Air Force in North Africa. Post-war, Reg Caldwell became a Master Seaman and died as Senior Master for Canada Steamship Lines.

His old friend George Lutz told me with trembling voice that he remembers Reg as "a pretty remarkable guy. He had a great deal of courage."

Bibliography

"A Dartmouth Sensation." *The Daily Acadian Recorder*. March 31 (1879): 3.

Adhar, George. *A Sketch of the Ministerial Labours of The Rev. Kenneth James Grant, D.D. Canadian Presbyterian Missionary; Pastor of the Susamachar Church; and Founder of the Trinidad Presbyterian College.* London: Bemrose and Sons Ltd., 1899.

Africville Genealogy Society, Black Cultural Centre for Nova Scotia, and the National Film Board. *Africville: A Spirit that Lives On.* Halifax: The Art Gallery of Mt. St. Vincent University, 1989.

Anselm, Sister Mary, (Irene Doyle). *The Antigonish Idea and Social Welfare.* Antigonish, NS: Saint Francis Xavier University Press, 1955.

Atlantic Broadcasters Ltd. Letter to Dept. of Transportation, Canada. Antigonish, NS: J. Clyde Nunn papers, private collection. Nov. 6 (1940).

"Babe Ruth Praises Halifax Man For Making Him A Great Ball Player." *The Halifax Herald*. August 21 (1920).

"Babes in Woods Lost 120 Years Ago" *Dartmouth Free Press*. Thursday, April 12, (1962): 1.

Balsor, Greta. "Once Thriving Community." *The Register*. April 12 (1995): 12.

Barris, Alex. *Front Page Challenge*. CBC Merchandising, 1981.

Beaglehole, J.C. *The Life of Captain James Cook*. California: Stanford University Press, 1974.

Berton, Pierre. *Vimy*. McClelland and Stewart, 1986.

Blois, Daniel. "Babes in the Wood." (song) Helen Creighton Collection, Nova Scotia Archives and Records Management.

Britten, Benjamin. *Letters from a Life; the selected letters and diaries of Benjamin Britten, 1913-1976.* Berkely: University of California Press, 1991.

Bullett, Gerald. *The English Galaxy of Shorter Poems.* London: J. M. Dent, 1933.

Burden, Arnold, and Andrew Safer. *Fifty Years of Emergencies: The Dramatic Life of a Country Doctor.* Hantsport, NS: Lancelot Press, 1991.

Campbell, Wilfred. *The Scotsman in Canada,* Vol. 1. Toronto: Musson Book Co., 1911.

"Captain Smith was a Windsor Man." *The Daily Echo*. 24 (1912): 1.

Carvajal, Doreen. "Yankee Finds Glory in Dixie." *The New York Times*. Nov. 13 (2000): E1, E4.

Chandler, Don. "A Remarkable Aircraft." (letter to the editor) *The Bulletin and The Progress Enterprise*. March 4 (1998).

Clark, Andrew H. " Titus Smith, Junior, and the Geography of Nova Scotia in 1801 and 1802." *Annals of the Association of American Geographers*, Vol. XLIV. December (1954): 291-314.

Coady, Rev. M.M. *The Social Significance of the Co-Operative Movement.* Antigonish, NS: Saint Francis Xavier University Press, 1955.

Collier, James Lincoln. *Duke Ellington*. Toronto: Collier Macmillan, 1991.

"Colonial Union, Dinner of Monday Night, Full Report on Speeches." *The British Colonist*, Vol. 8 No. 3. September 15 (1864).

Cousins, Leone Banks. "Woman of the Year-1842: The Story or Eliza Ruggles Raymond and Mutiny on the Slave Ship Amistad." *The Nova Scotia Historical Quarterly*, Vol. 6 No. 4.

Creamer, Robert. *Babe: The Legend Comes to Life*. New York: Simon and Schuster, 1992.

Crooker, William. *Oak Island: one of the world's most baffling mysteries*. Halifax, NS: Nimbus, 1993.

Dancocks, Daniel G. *Spearhead to Victory : Canada and the Great War*. Edmonton: Hurtig, 1987.

Dosseter, J.B., K.J. MacKinnon, J.C. Luke, R.O. Morgan, J.C. Beck. "Renal Transplantation Between Identical Twins." *The Lancet 2* (1960): 572-577.

Dow, Leslie Smith. *Anna Leonowens: A Life Beyond the King and I*. Nova Scotia: Pottersfield Press, 1991.

"Dr. McDonald." *The Nova Scotian*. January 4 (1847): 7.

"Earth From Nova Scotia Is Deposited In Scotland." *Mail Star*. Wednesday, Oct. 21 (1953): 6.

Ellington, Edward Kennedy. *Music is My Mistress*. Garden City, NY: Doubleday, 1973.

Ellington, Mercer, and Stanley Dance. *Duke Ellington in Person: an intimate memoir by Mercer Ellington*. New York: Houghton Mifflin Co., 1978.

Evans, Millie, and Eric Mullen. *Oak Island*. Four East Publishing, 1984.

Fillmore, Stanley, and R.W. Sandilands. *The Chartmakers; a history of nautical surveying in Canada*. Canadian Hydrographic Service, 1983.

Fingard, Judith. *The Dark Side of Life in Victorian Halifax*. Porter's Lake, NS: Pottersfield Press, 1989.

Finnan, Mark. *Oak Island Secrets*. Halifax, NS: Formac, 1997.

Fraser, Mary L. *Folklore of Nova Scotia*. Antigonish, NS: Formac Ltd., 1975.

Fuller, Alfred C. and Spence Hartzell. *A Foot in the Door: The Life Appraisal of the Original Fuller Brush Man as Told to Hartzell Spence*. New York: McGraw-Hill Book Company, Inc, 1960.

Fun at Five. Radio Broadcast narr. J. Clyde Nunn and Percy Baker. CJFX Radio. Mar. 25 1968.

Gallagher, Janice. "Murray Wood, Oldest Surviving Munchkin From Oz." *The Miami Herald*. Sept. 27 (1999): 4B.

Gaudet, Leonard W. *Gaudet Genealogy; Ancestors of Leonard William Gaudet*. Dartmouth: unpublished, 1997.

Gaudet, Leonard W., and Geoffrey Plank. *Jacques Maurice Vigneau and the Meaning of Acadian Neutrality*. (Draft) Cincinatti: University of Cincinatti.

Giefler, Patricia. *Valour Remembered: Canada and the First World War, 1918 - Nov 11 1978*. Ottawa: Minister of Supply and Services, 1980.

"Green Room Gossip." *The Sydney Post*. February 11 (1922).

Hammond, John Winthrop. "A Tribute to Walter D'Arcy Ryan." *The General Electric Review*. April (1934): 15.

Hill, Shirley Elizabeth. "The Ups and Downs of Andrew's Zoo." *The Westender*. May (1985): 3, 6.

Hinds, Barbara. *The Lost Patrol: the story of Inspector Francis J. Fitzgerald's final patrol as an officer of the Royal North West Mounted Police*. Halifax, NS: Friends of the Public Gardens, 1994.

"Honor Ties Which Bind New Scotland To Old." *Halifax Herald*. Oct. 21 (1953): 1.

"The Horses were Saved by Children." Halifax, Nova Scotia: Nova Scotia Museum.

Howell, Colin. *Northern Sandlots: A social history of Maritime baseball*. Toronto: Univ. of Toronto Press, 1995.

Howell, Colin. "The Man Who Taught the Bambino." *All I Thought About was Baseball; Writings on a Canadian Pastime*. Ed. Humber, William and John St. James. Toronto: Univ. of Toronto Press, 1996.

Innes, Lorna. "Dec. 21-28, 1955: that was the week." *Mail Star*. Dec. 28 (1985).

"The Inventions that Changed the World." *Reader's Digest*. (1982): 151.

Jewell, Derek. *Duke: A Portrait of Duke Ellington*. New York: W.W. Norton and Co. Inc., 1977.

Johnston, Doug. *From Airgunner to Prisoner of War: the true story of a young banker, his wartime experiences including forty missions and his months as a prisoner of war*. Toronto: Johnston/McDowell, 1994.

Johnston, Ian. "Help Solve Mystery of Halifax Munchkin." *The Daily News*. April 12 (2000): 30.

Kilbracken, John. *Bring Back My Stringbag: Swordfish Pilot at War 1940-1945*. London: Leo Cooper, 1996.

Lacey, Pat. *Master of the Titanic*. Long Preston: Magna Large Print Books, 1997.

"Lakes, salt marshes, and the narrow green strip: some historic buildings in Dartmouth and Halifax County's eastern shore." Halifax, NS: Heritage Trust of Nova Scotia, 1979.

Lawson, Mrs. William (Mary Jane Katzman). *History of the Townships of Dartmouth, Preston and Lawrencetown: Halifax County, N.S* Ed. Harry Piers. Bellville, Ontario: Mika Studio, 1972.

Legget, Robert F. *Canadian Consulting Engineer*. Don Mills, ON: Southam Business Publications. May (1978): 46-47.

Lively, Arleen. "Hollywood Movie Has Real Life Local Character." *The Register*. February 18 (1998): 12.

"Lower Cove Resident Recalls Heroic Event" *The Citizen*. Amherst, NS. May 1 (1982): 1.

MacDermot, T.W.L. *The Seventh*. Montreal: The Seventh Canadian Siege Battery Assoc.

MacDonald, J.J. *The Nova Scotia Post: its offices, masters and marks, 1700-1867*. Toronto: Unitrade Press, 1985.

Martin, J.P. *Stories of Dartmouth: the babes in the wood, with a road guide to the graves of the children at Woodlawn*. Halifax, 1944. (missing publisher... is this an article or a book?)

Matte, James Allen. *Forensic Psychophysiology Using the Polygraph*. Williamsdale, NY: J.A.M. Publications, 1996.

McLauchlan, Laura. "Nova Scotia's First Female Woods Guide." *The Coast Guard*. Feb. 8 (2000): 5A.

McVicar, Paul. *The Life and Times of 95 King Street: 1815-1996; An Informal History of the Mystery House*. Dartmouth, NS: (private publication), 1996.

Miller, Harry H. "An Incident of the Spanish-American war." *Noel Shore Journal*. Winter (1900).

Milnes, Arthur. "The Loss of a Leader." *The Kingston Whig Standard*. June 10 (2000): 2.

Moon, Barbara. "Double Jeopardy; the Johnson twins' sunny brush with tragedy." *MacLean's*. July 16 (1960): 14.

Moosai-Maharaj, S. "One Hundred Years After 1870." Address delivered at Susamachar Church, San Fernando, Trinidad, West Indies. November 22, 1970.

Morgan, Robert J. "Separatism in Cape Breton." Speech at Baddeck Community Centre, Nova Scotia, Feb 19, 2000.

Morrison, James H and James Moreira. *Tempered By Rum: Rum in the History of the Maritime Provinces*. Porter's Lake, NS: Pottersfield Press, 1988.

Moyles, R. Gordon. *The blood and fire in Canada : a history of the Salvation Army in the Dominion, 1882-1976*. Toronto: P. Martin Associates, 1977.

Mulholland, Jill. "The Illumination of the Panama Pacific International Exposition; San Francisco, 1915." Princeton, NJ. Unpublished.

National Film Board. "Africville: A Spirit that Lives on." With the Art Gallery of Mt. St. Vincent U., Africville Genealogy Society, and Black Cultural Centre for Nova Scotia.

"New Antigonish Radio Station Goes On Air." *The Halifax Herald*. March 24 (1943).

The New Illustrated Science and Invention Encyclopedia, Vol. 15. New York: Marshall Cavenish, 1987.

Nickerson, Alex. "MacDonald was Star in Silent Pictures." *Halifax Chronicle Herald*. Nov. 24 (1978).

"No Passport For Strasser Is Decision." *Chronicle Herald*. January 15 (1949).

North, Dick. *The Lost Patrol: The Mounties' Yukon Tragedy*. Anchorage: Alaska Northwest Pub. Co., 1978.

Nunn, Bruce. "Life was his Podium: A Biography of J. Clyde Nunn." Unpublished essay. Antigonish, NS: St. Francis Xavier University. April (1984).

Pachai, Bridglal. *Blacks*. Halifax, NS: Nimbus Publishing, 1996.

Parks, Gordon. "A Jazz of Their Own." *Vanity Fair*. May (1999): 188-196.

Piers, Harry. "Titus Smith, 'The Dutch Village Philosopher', Pioneer Naturalist of Nova Scotia, 1768-1850." *NS Institute of Science*. July (1938).

Pirone, Dorothy Ruth and Chris Martens. *My Dad, The Babe; Growing up with an American Hero*. Boston: Quinlan Press, 1988.

"Played 'Santa' for Forty Years." *War Cry* (Toronto). Christmas (1955).

"Pride of Sydney at the Strand." *The Sydney Post*. August 23 (1922).

Punch, Terrence M. "Maple Sugar and Cabbages: The Philosophy of the Dutch Village Philosopher." *Nova Scotia Historical Quarterly*, Vol. 8. (1978).

"Ragan, David." *Who's Who in Hollywood; The Largest Cast of Film Personalities Ever Assembled*, Vol. 2. New York: Facts on File, 1992.

Reed, Douglas. *The Story of Otto Strasser and the Black Front*. Boston: Houghton Mifflin Co., 1940.

"Remember the Message!" *War Cry*, Salvation Army. 1981.

Richardson, Deborah. "The Duke at 100." *Daybreak Express*. (Newsletter of the Archives Center, National Museum of American History, Smithsonian Institution, Washington, D.C.) Spring (1999): 1, 6.

Rientis, Rex. *James Cook*. London: Oxford University Press, 1969.

Rigli, Ron. "Follow the Yellow Brick Road." *Autograph Times*. Feb. (2000): 20.

Ringle, Ken. "A Canadian in the Eye of the Storm." *The Ottawa Citizen*. Dec. 23 (2000): B7.

Roué, Joan E. *A Spirit Deep Whithin: Naval Architect W.J. Roué and the Bluenose Story*. Hantsport, NS: Lancelot Press, 1994.

Rowell, John Richard. "An Intellectual in Politics; Norman Rogers as an Intellectual and Minister of Labour: 1929-1939." (A thesis submitted to the Department of History in conformity with the requirements for the degree of Master of Arts.) Kingston, ON: Queen's University, 1978.

Royal Northwest Mounted Police. *Reports and Other Papers relating to the McPherson-Dawson police patrol — winter 1910-1911 — and the death of Inspector Francis J. Fitzgerald and all members of the patrol*. Ottawa: King's Printer, 1911.

Ruggles family Bible, annotated. Private Collection of Joel Heddington: Halifax, NS.

Schrepfer, Rev. Luke. *Pioneer Monks in Nova Scotia*. Monastery, NS: St. Augustine's Monastery, 1947.

"Sentences Imposed On Amherst Men." *Amherst Daily News*. May 20 (1926).

Singer, David. "Firefighting in Halifax: From 1754-1917." *The Senior's Advocate*, Vol. 9, No. 6. Dec-Jan (1992): 13.

Smith, Titus. "Mineralogy." Transcript of a lecture delivered by Titus Smith to Halifax Mechanics' Institute, Mar. 5, 1834. Halifax Mechanics' Institute, 1834.

Sneden, Robert Knox. *Eye of the Storm*. Ed. Bryan, Charles F. Jr. and Nelson D. Lankford. New York: Free Press, 2000.

Stachura, Peter D. *Gregor Strasser and the Rise of Nazism*. London: George Allen and Unwin, 1983.

Stehelin, Paul H. *The Electric City: The Stehelins of New France*. Hantsport, NS: Lancelot Press, 1983.

Stickney, G. II. "Walter D'Arcy Ryan." *Magazine of Light*. Summer (1934): 9.

"Still Giving Leadership In Germany Says Strasser." *Chronicle Herald*. January 12 (1949).

"Strange Move Says Strasser Of Book Ban." *Chronicle Herald*. January 26 (1949).

"Strasser's Book Banned from Zone." *Chronicle Herald*. January 22 (1949).

"Strasser En Route To Bridgetown." *Chronicle Herald*. September 1 (1949).

"Strasser's Plans Meet Opposition." *Chronicle Herald*. February 13 (1952).

Strasser, Otto. *Hitler and I*. London: Jonathan Cape, 1940.

"They Brought Fame to Noel Shore." *Chronicle Herald*. December 28 (1963): 13.

"Trapped on Reef As Tide Rises, Trio Is Rescued" *Halifax Herald*. April 25 (1948).

"U.S. General Warns Against Plans of Dr. Otto Strasser." Chronicle Herald. January 11 (1949).

"W.D. Ryan Died Mar. 14 After Serving 38 Years." *Schenectady World News*, a newsletter of General Electric Co. March 23 (1934): 2.

Waite, Peter B. *The Life and Times of Confederation: 1864-1867; Politics, Newspapers, and the Union of British North America*. Toronto: University of Toronto Press, 1962.

Waite, Peter B. *Macdonald: His Life and World*. McGraw-Hill Ryerson Limited, 1975. (location missing)

"Wallace MacDonald in Movies." *Sydney Daily Post*. June 12 (1918).

Walsh, Paul. *Political Profiles: Premiers of Nova Scotia*. Halifax, NS: Nimbus Publishing, 1986.

Wells, Paul. "Reminiscing in Tempo." *The National Post*. April 24 (1999): Weekend Post Arts, 1.

Who Was Who in America 1961-1968, Vol. 4. Chicago: Marquis Inc., 1968.

"Willard Miller, 81, Dies; Won Medal of Honor." *Washington Star* . March 3 (1959).

Williston, Floyd. *Johnny Miles, Nova Scotia's Marathon King*. Halifax, NS: Nimbus Publishing, 1990.

Wilson, Keith. "Amore De Cosmos." Faculty of Education, University of Manitoba, 1985.

Wrather, W.E. "Memorial to Donald Francis MacDonald." Proceedings Volume of the Geographical Society of America; Annual Report for 1949. June (1950): 197-200.

Online Resources

Amistad America
http://www.amistadamerica.org/main/welcome.html

Archives Centre: Earl S. Tupper Papers
http://americanhistory.si.edu/archives/d8470b.htm

"Epileptic", "Fainting", "Nervous" Or "Stiff Legged" Goats
http://lazybranch.tripod.com/lbrepileptic.html

Fainting Goats
http://www-personal.umich.edu/~jimknapp/goats.html

The Fairey Swordfish: a British biplane
http://vectorsite.tripod.com/avsword.html

Folk Songs of Old England: Babes in the Wood
http://www.informatik.uni-hamburg.de/~zierke/steeleye.span/songs/
babesinthewood.html

Illuminating Engineering Society of North America
http://www.iesna.org

International Fainting Goat Association
http://www.faintinggoat.com

The Internet Movie Database
http://us.imdb.com

John Kilbracken and Killegar, family home of the Godleys
http://homepage.tinet.ie/~carrigallen/killegar.html

LineOne news: Lord Kilbracken and the end of the House of Lords
http://www.lineone.net/express/99/11/12/news/n2720lords-d.html

Manwoman's Swastika page
http://www.manwoman.net

National Maritime Museum
http://www.nmm.ac.uk

Origins of the Civil War Conflict
http://www.ilt.columbia.edu/k12/history/gb/origin.html

The Stehelin's "Electric City"
http://collections.ic.gc.ca/electric

The Swastika and the Nazis
http://www.intelinet.org/swastika/swastika_intro.htm

Veterans Affairs Canada
http://www.vac-acc.gc.ca

Virginia Historical Society: Union Private Robert K. Sneden
http://vahistorical.org/news/sneden_news.htm